THE ART OF BEING A HAPPILY MARRIED MAN

HOW TO BUILD A JOYFUL, PASSIONATE, PURPOSE-FILLED, FAITH-FOCUSED RELATIONSHIP THAT WILL LAST.

MEB WEST

JENNY WEST

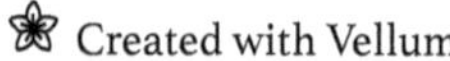 Created with Vellum

To Jenny:

My eternal companion - The one and only woman in the universe who can make me blush, curl my toes, humble me, and give me butterflies...all with one look. Thank you for your patience, grace, humor, and stubbornness. It is only because of you that this book and anything else important in my life exists. Thank you for giving me the opportunity to try and be the man you have always deserved. More than that, thanks for being so patient and forgiving as you watch me repeatedly fail to achieve that goal. Just think of me...

To Brooke:

May this serve as an enduring reminder that - despite the challenges life threw at us - your parents were, are, and will forever remain madly in love and eternally unbreakable. I wish you a double portion of the happiness we share.

CONTENTS

INTRODUCTION

Marriage is one of life's most incredible adventures – part rollercoaster, part road trip. There are days you feel like the perfect team and other days when you're arguing about whose turn it is to take the dog out (Spoiler Alert: it's probably always your turn). Let's  face it: being married is fantastic, but it's not always easy.

If you've ever found yourself scratching your head, wondering how you went from romantic getaways to debates about proper dishwasher-loading techniques, you're not alone. Every husband has been there – facing the challenge of figuring out what it takes to make a good marriage truly great (Heck, half the time, I'm wondering if today's the day she'll finally be fed up with my antics and start packing the car!).

The good news? You don't need to have all the answers, but you *do* need to have a plan. And that's where this book comes in. *The Art of Being a Happily Married Man* is your no-nonsense guide to building a joyful, passionate, and purpose-filled marriage – a relationship you can brag about to your friends without them rolling their eyes and uninviting you from next season's hunting trip.

A Marriage Built to Last

When I married Jenny over 33 years ago, I thought I had it all figured out. It would be a gross understatement to say that I did not. Not even close. Contrary to what my 18-year-old self would tell you, I had nothing figured out. Like most newlyweds, we were optimistic, starry-eyed, and utterly clueless about what it would take to make our relationship thrive over decades.

Then – as it does – life happened. We had to navigate financial struggles, career pressures, and the unique challenges of being a military family – like learning how not to attempt to pack in a year's worth of marriage between back-to-back deployments (it doesn't work, trust me). It wasn't always smooth sailing, but those bumps in the road taught us something important: a strong marriage isn't something you stumble into. It's something you build, one choice at a time. Sometimes it's ugly, often it's hard, but it can also be *SO* rewarding.

And while I've worn many hats in my life – a retired U.S. Army Senior Leader, a seasoned security consultant, and a guy who knows how to make the meanest salsa this side of the Rio Grande – my most rewarding role has been that of a husband. Not because I've been perfect at it (far from it) but because I've learned how to show up, grow up, and do the work. And let's be honest with each other from the start; it is work. Darn, hard work.

Please don't think I'm some marriage guru with fancy schooling on this subject. I'm not. When it comes to marriage, I graduated *Suma Cum Laude* from the University of Hard Knocks (Go Bull-heads!). Frankly, I feel like somewhat of a fraud even writing this book. I've made about every mistake you can make in a marriage. Every. Single. One. That we are still married after 33 years is solely due to Jenny's determination, grit, grace, and (often) down-right stubbornness. I would have quit on me years ago. But here we are, collaborating on a book that speaks to being happily married. If that isn't a testament to God's grace and what hard work and mutual dedication can bring, I don't know what is. This book is written based on what I learned works after countless years of repeatedly doing things that didn't work. Learn from my mistakes and pray you've married someone as strong and patient as I did.

A Shared Journey

Every husband struggles with the same questions at some point:

- "How can I talk to her about my stress without sounding like a mess?"
- "Is there a way to keep the romance alive when you're exhausted by 9 PM?"
- "If she doesn't want me to fix it, do I have to listen to her complain about it?"

- "How hard is it to put the TV remote back where you found it?"

This book tackles those questions and more (except the TV remote question...which will remain a mystery for the ages). Whether you're looking to improve communication, reignite intimacy, or figure out how to parent as a united front, you'll find the tools you need here.

But this isn't just about fixing problems. It's about building something extraordinary – a marriage that makes you feel proud, supported, and connected every day.

Why This Book Is Different

Here's the deal: I don't do fluff. This book is packed with **practical, actionable steps** – the type of advice you can use today without needing a PhD in relationship studies. I've also sprinkled in plenty of real-life examples and scenarios (yes, some of them embarrassingly personal) so you know you're not the only one navigating the challenges of married life.

And let's not forget the humor. Life's too short to take yourself too seriously. If you can't laugh about some of the ridiculous moments marriage throws your way, you're missing out on half the fun.

It's also different because you will hear a woman's honest perspective – one who doesn't have skin in the game of keeping the peace in your marriage. Jenny has graciously agreed to share her brutally honest perspective that – if we play our cards right – might teach us ALL a thing or two that a testosterone-fueled binge book might otherwise find lacking.

You may want to consider bringing your wife into your study of this book. You may find it a much more holistic adventure involving an added level of mutual learning and growth. You can bounce Jenny's opinion off of your wife's. Does she agree or disagree with the female perspective? Take notes on your wife's feedback as you work through the book together...those are priceless golden nuggets.

Your Role

This book is for you, the guy ready to take his marriage from "pretty good" to "better than I could have imagined." No matter where you're starting from, there's something here for you. You don't need to be perfect (look at me!), but you do need to show up, take action, and be willing to grow. That may get a little uncomfortable.

Trigger warning: we will be talking about "mushy stuff" like feelings, love, romance, and communication. I'm going to ask you to actually do some reflection and self-assessment. So go out and swing a hammer, throw some weights around the gym, or rev an engine a time or two. Once the testosterone machine has been sufficiently fed, strap in and get ready to do some of the most challenging, most uncomfortable, most rewarding work you'll ever do.

Jenny's Comments

To be fair, we are not formally educated in the Mental Health or Marriage Counseling space. However, we have practical, real-world experience in just about every topic and problem that attacks a marriage from the inside and out. The military has sent us to various marriage retreats, we have attended many sessions of couples counseling, and we've attended marriage conferences, workshops and retreats throughout the United States. We've read many marriage books together that have helped teach us necessary communication skills. Since March 16, 1991, we have been a part of a connection with each other that has become something brand new and completely unexpected.

That said, it does not surprise me at all that Meb wanted to write this book. He is a teacher at heart and loves to share his knowledge with whoever wants or needs it. He has done the work, through blood, sweat, and many, many tears, to become the man that he is today. The "married" man he is today is more loving, more empathetic, more caring, more nurturing, God-fearing, mind-reading, and finally seems to have his priorities in the right order. We've been through hell and back together to get here, yet here we are...in our undies at the kitchen table, eating leftover spaghetti and writing a book about our journey with marriage.

Husbands, it does not matter what you have done in the past. It is NEVER too late to turn things around and make necessary changes in your life that matter. You can become the husband and leader in your home that your family needs you to be, regardless of any actions that you may have taken to destroy those titles. You must be willing to change. You must be willing to get to know your wife intimately, in ALL the ways. You must be willing to ask questions of yourself and of her and to get to know one another on a much deeper level. If you can create a connection with God and incorporate Him and Jesus Christ's atonement into your marriage, then that will take it to another level. We will talk more about this subject in another chapter, as I can already see many of you rolling your eyes and wanting to throw the book out now. This is not to say that a great marriage requires a specific type of religion. It's simply a data point. Connecting with a community of others who also regard marriage as important and necessary, as well as accepting that there is a higher power that can give us peace and teach us how to love more fully, can only benefit and support our family unit and functions. Please continue to give this book a chance and hear us out. You may just learn something, and that something may save your marriage or increase your connection for a much more rewarding relationship.

Wives, it does not matter what your husband has done in the past. If he is looking, you square in the eyes and telling you that he sincerely wants to create a much more meaningful connection with you now, grab that opportunity with both hands, hold onto it tightly, and don't ever let go! We must be willing to forgive. We must be willing to open our minds to something new and open our hearts (YIKES!) to his love again and again. If your man is reading this book, trust me, there IS a chance. You can get to a life that you love together. I know that nothing is impossible to work through to get where you've always wanted, hoped, and wished for in your marriage.

Ready to Begin?

By the end of this book, you'll have a toolkit to create the kind of marriage that feels like a partnership, not a project. You'll walk away with real confidence and maybe even a few new inside jokes with your wife.

Let's get started – our best days as happily married men are ahead of us.

CHAPTER 1
YOU MEAN I HAVE TO TALK AND LISTEN?

MASTERING COMMUNICATION FOR CONNECTION

If marriage is a dance, communication is the music. And let's be honest – most of us guys aren't exactly waltzing through conversations. It's more like awkwardly stepping on each other's toes and hoping for the best. No, that's not accurate enough. We're more like a group of Amish barn raisers at a break-dancing competition. But here's the truth: if you can master communication, you'll unlock the secret sauce of a happy marriage.

The good news? You don't need to become a poet or a mind reader. You just need to learn a few simple tools to connect better, express yourself clearly, and actually understand (not just hear) what your wife is trying to say (HINT: "Fine" is NEVER an accurate depiction of her opinion, nor is it EVER an appropriate response to any question, no matter the topic of conversation!).

Active Listening: The Key to Understanding

Listening is the foundation of communication. But let's be real: most of us think we're better listeners than we actually are. It's not enough to nod and say "uh-huh" while secretly replaying last night's sports highlights in your head. Active listening requires intention, focus, and – brace yourself – effort.

The Three Pillars of Active Listening

1. Eye Contact and Body Language: You've probably heard it before, but it bears repeating: put down the phone and pause the game. I know it's hard. Instagram is calling, the meme just posted in the group chat is hilarious, and our fantasy player is about to go crazy. But nothing says, "You're important to me," like giving your wife your full attention. Sit up straight, make eye contact, and lean in slightly to show you're engaged (don't forget to blink, or it will get really creepy, really quick!). Think of yourself as an investigative reporter: curious, attentive, and ready to uncover the juicy details. I'm telling you, this is your wife's equivalent of coming into the bedroom in sexy lingerie.

WARNING: If this hasn't been in your toolbox up to this point, expect that it may go a little rough at first. She may think you're making fun of her, or it may shock her into silence. Just be patient and consistent. If you do, she'll eventually warm up to the fact that she's married to the man of her dreams.

2. *Reflective Listening:* This isn't about being a parrot. When she says, "I feel like we never spend time together," don't just repeat, "You feel like we never spend time together." Try adding a little extra, like, "You're feeling like we've been too busy lately, and it's bothering you. Did I get that right?" This small tweak lets her know you're really hearing her *and care* that you are understanding correctly. It's sometimes helpful during long conversations to offer a reflective listening "summary" during natural pauses in the conversation. This tells her 1) you are actually listening, and 2) you get the "so what?" of it all up to this point. Don't overdo this, though, as no one likes to be interrupted or lose their train of thought.

3. *Avoiding Interruptions:* Speaking of interruptions, guys, I know it's tempting to jump in with a solution the second you hear a problem. But trust me, she's not looking for Captain Fix-It (I don't know why either…it's gotta be one of those "Mars/Venus" things). Most of the time, she just wants you to *listen*. To understand her. To be her hype crew. To tell her she's right or not crazy. To agree that her best friend crossed the line or her coworker was a jerk. Bite your tongue, take a deep breath, and let her finish. There's a time for solutions, and it's not while she's venting.

In fact, in a time where she is NOT telling you about a problem, you should have a chat with her. Together, come up with a phrase, question, or word that lets you know whether she wants you to help _solve_ or help _soothe_. One requires a solution. The other requires nothing but your time and undivided attention.

Practice Makes Perfect

Think you've got this active listening thing down? Test yourself with these exercises:

The Listening Game: Take turns sharing something about your day while the other listens without interrupting. Then, summarize what the other person said.

Silent Countdown: When you feel the urge to interject, count to three in your head before speaking. This will give her space to finish her thoughts.

The Empathy Factor

Listening isn't just about hearing words; it's about understanding emotions. If she's venting about her boss, she doesn't want to hear, "Well, have you tried being more assertive?" Start with something empathetic, like, "That sounds tough. I can see why you're frustrated." or "Man, if that had happened to me, I'm not sure how it would have made me feel. How did it make you feel?" Trust me, that small shift changes everything.

I've also found that in these moments, it is NOT helpful to try and draw a comparison to a similar situation in your life. You run the risk of 1) being perceived as hijacking the conversation and making it about you or 2) being perceived as "not getting it" because the situation you shared did not have the nuances of what she was trying to share with you.

What if this fails? Just remember this: At a bare minimum, nod, maintain eye contact, keep a neutral facial expression, and – <u>under no circumstances</u> - bring up the game you're missing or ask her to wait until the commercial.

Expressing Emotions Clearly and Confidently

Most of us grew up in a world where "show no weakness" was the golden rule. Unfortunately, that doesn't translate well to marriage. Your wife doesn't need you to be a stoic statue. Her definition of what a "man" is, is very different than yours. She needs you to be real, even if that means admitting you're stressed, scared, or (gulp) wrong.

Why "I Feel" or "I Perceive" Statements Work

Let's say you're frustrated because your wife made plans without checking in first. Instead of saying, "You never ask me before scheduling things!" (instant fight), try this:

State how you feel: "I feel frustrated..."

Explain why: "...because I didn't know we were having company, and I was hoping to relax."

Ask for what you need: "...so next time, would it be okay if we check in with each other before making plans?"

See the difference? It's not about assigning blame; it's about sharing your perspective. When you say, "I feel" or "I perceive," it takes the blame off her or her action and puts the blame on how you processed it. Plus, it makes you sound like a relationship Yoda.

Expanding Your Emotional Toolbox

Saying, "I'm fine" or "I'm good," is fine in a conversation with your gym workout buddy. But it doesn't cut it with your wife. Your wife needs to know what's really going on. If your emotional vocabulary feels like it's stuck in preschool, start expanding it. Here are some options:

Instead of "mad," try "frustrated," "annoyed," or "disappointed."

Instead of "happy," try "content," "excited," or "grateful."

Instead of "sad," try "discouraged," "lonely," or "disheartened."

Instead of "stressed," try "overwhelmed," "tense," "uneasy," or "pressured."

Instead of "angry," try "irritated," "resentful," "betrayed," or "offended."

Instead of "worried," try "anxious," "apprehensive," "nervous," or "concerned."

Instead of "tired," try "drained," "fatigued," "unmotivated," or "exhausted."

Instead of "confused," try "uncertain," "torn," "disoriented," or "puzzled."

Instead of "lonely," try "isolated," "disconnected," "neglected," or "unseen."

Instead of "embarrassed," try "self-conscious," "ashamed," or "exposed."

Instead of "excited," try "elated," "thrilled," "hopeful," or "eager."

Instead of "hurt," try "offended," "disrespected," "heartbroken," or "let down."

Practice Makes Progress

Here's how to get comfortable expressing emotions:

Journaling: Spend five minutes a day writing down what you're feeling and why (Yes, I'm serious. And yes, I told you things were going to get "mushy." No one has to see it, and it's a great way to practice).

Daily Check-Ins: At the end of each day, share one thing that made you happy, one thing that frustrated you, and one thing you're grateful for. Try to use different descriptive words each time you talk about your emotions.

Navigating Difficult Conversations with Ease

Anyone can do fairly well talking to someone else when the topic is easy or if there is no pressure. But one of the most critical components of effective marital communication is the "art of the difficult conversation," i.e., arguing. This topic is so important that it deserves its own chapter (Chapter 2 – next). So, for the time being, let's just put a pin in it.

Non-Verbal Communication: Reading Between the Lines

Let's not kid ourselves – most communication isn't verbal. The fancy statistic that is quoted all the time is that out of the three elements that convey 100% of a message, only 7% are words, 38% are tone, and a whopping 55% are body language.

Don't believe me? Try this little experiment: Say, "Have a nice day". Now, without changing the words, say the same phrase but have it actually mean, "Go screw yourself and have a horrible day." It's surprisingly easy to do.

Our brothers and sisters south of the Mason-Dixon line have perfected this art with the phrase, "Bless your heart." And – for all you Army readers – we can have the word "huah," literally mean 20+ different things, depending on our tone and body language.

The point is this: Yes, our words matter, but statistically, our tone and body language matter _at least_ 10x more. Those of us who are stumped by the "What did I say?" dilemma have failed to remember this concept. Your wife picks up on your tone, your expressions, and even that subtle "I'm trying to escape this conversation" body shift. Mastering non-verbal cues is like unlocking the cheat codes of communication.

Sending the Right Signals – Let's review some specific aspects of body language.

Eye Contact – The Window to Connection: Maintaining comfortable eye contact shows your wife that you're fully present and engaged. It builds trust and creates a sense of intimacy. Avoid the "glazed over" look or accidentally staring too intensely like you're interrogating them – it's all about balance.

Open Posture – The "I Care" Move: Face her directly, uncross your arms and legs. Leaning slightly toward her shows interest and attentiveness. It's a way of physically saying, "I'm here with you." Don't lean too far; you might end up in her lap – adorable in movies, awkward at the dinner table.

Head Tilts – The "I'm Listening" Signal: Tilting your head slightly while she is speaking shows curiosity and engagement. It's a subtle way of saying, "I'm really paying attention to you." Just be careful – overdo the head tilt move, and you'll look like you're trying out to be the new RCA dog mascot.

Nods of Agreement – The Silent "I'm With You": A well-timed nod shows her that you're following along and agree with what she's saying. It's like a nonverbal high-five. Just make sure you're listening attentively. The last thing you want to do is give a subtle nod when she asks, "That doesn't make me crazy, does it?" You've been warned. Also, don't overdo this technique to the point that you look like you're trying to win a bobblehead competition.

Facial Expressions – The Smile Says It All: Your face tells a story, whether you intend it to or not. A warm smile, a raised eyebrow of curiosity, or a nod of encouragement can make her feel valued. Just keep the "are-you-serious-right-now?" eye rolls to a minimum.

Mirroring – The Subtle Sync-Up: Mirroring your wife's body language (subtly!) signals that you're on the same wavelength. It creates a subconscious feeling of connection. But don't overdo it, or she'll think you're auditioning for a mime troupe. No one likes mimes, and there's a reason for it.

Slow Movements – The Measured and Collected Approach: Slow, intentional movements signal patience and thoughtfulness. Quick, jerky movements can make you seem anxious or irritated, even if you're not. Again, overdoing this has consequences. Don't use this technique so effectively that your wife calls 911 because she thinks you have slipped into a life-threatening medical condition.

Relaxed Hands – The Calm Communicator: Keeping your hands relaxed and open communicates ease and approachability. Crossed arms or clenched fists can signal tension – even if you're not upset. There's really no way to overdo this, but don't make it too obvious. If every time you start to get frustrated, you shove your hands in your pockets; you may be sending a subliminal message that you're playing with something that you shouldn't be playing with.

Gentle Touch – The Nonverbal Hug: A light touch on the hand, arm, or shoulder can instantly diffuse tension, show empathy, and reassure her. It's like a tiny, physical "I'm here for you." Don't be overly dramatic with this, like Scarlet O'Hara in *Gone with the Wind.* Also, be cautious of sending the wrong message with your "gentle touch." If done incorrectly, you could subliminally (or consciously) send the message that you want to get amorous...which isn't appropriate when she's telling you about an argument she had with her mom.

Laughing Together - The Joyful Bond: Laughter is a form of body language that breaks down walls and creates instant connection. Sharing a giggle, even over something silly, strengthens your relationship. Don't fake the laugh and come across as disingenuous. That will do more harm than good. Also, (and this is important) watch laughing while you're drinking anything. Hot chocolate coming out of the nose might make things even more funny, but it hurts really bad and isn't worth it in the long run.

Practice Makes Perfect

Here's an exercise you can do to get better at using your body language and tone to send your intended message.

Get in front of a mirror (don't just sit there rolling your eyes...go do it, it's important!) and practice saying the following phrase:

"I hear you."

Use the elements of body language we reviewed above to send various messages, such as humor, understanding, sarcasm, etc. Then, take it to the next level. Figure out how to use your facial expressions, tone, and gestures to come across as more genuine or authentic.

Building Emotional Intelligence Together

If communication is the music of marriage, Emotional Intelligence (EI) is the amplifier. It takes good communication and makes it great. Emotional intelligence is about two equally important things that must be done simultaneously: 1) managing your own feelings and 2) *accurately* tuning into your wife's feelings. We've subtly been talking about emotional intelligence throughout this chapter, but if you've been skipping around, let's review some of EI's important aspects.

Self-awareness – Knowing Thyself: Self-awareness is understanding your own emotions and recognizing how they impact your wife. It's realizing when you're cranky because you're hungry, not because she left the toothpaste cap off (again). There's a reason that "hangry" is a word.

This is one that I struggle with quite a bit. I have significant anxiety attacks and mild panic disorder in certain situations. In crowds, certain social situations, or during times when I'm really trying to concentrate, my communication skills drop *way* off. I come across as frustrated, irritated, or downright enraged. Sometimes, I'll literally just shut down and retreat inside of myself. If left unregulated, I can be a major you-know-what to Jenny. I have literally bit her head off when she approached me with a funny story because I was "in the zone" of deep concentration (talk about feeling like a jerk!). If I can be mindful of this personality quirk, I can try to be more present and aware of my verbal and nonverbal communication with Jenny. Often, I'll stop, take a deep breath to reset, and then interact with her to try and regulate those unintentional, knee-jerk responses. The added benefit is that when Jenny notices me doing this, she has learned to recognize the sign and give me a bit of grace if I'm not completely on my game.

Empathy – Walking in Their Shoes (Even If They're Psychedelic, Fuzzy Ugg Slippers): Empathy is about understanding your wife's feelings, even when they're not outright saying them. It's noticing that her "I'm fine" is code for "I've had a terrible day, and I need a hug." As mentioned before, it's important to know when it's appropriate to <u>solve</u> and (more likely) when it's appropriate to <u>soothe</u>. Cool-guy tip from a used-to-be cool guy: "Sucks to be you!" is not an appropriately empathetic response, and the sarcasm falls as flat as a fart in church.

Emotional Regulation – Keeping Your Cool: Emotional regulation is about managing your responses so you don't overreact when things get tough. It's the difference between calmly discussing a problem and storming out like a soap opera character. This is sometimes called the "Nobody's dying" perspective. In the grand scheme of things, is what is currently on the docket _really_ that big of a deal? A week from now, would this issue still be worth the argument? If the answer is no, try and find a way to tone it down a notch.

As guys, we typically struggle with this one. We have a lot of issues that we will "fall on the sword" over. We have standards to uphold, morals to defend, and principles that can't be compromised. It is important to differentiate our "societal self" from our "husband self." In society, there are a lot of threats to our morality, standards, and principles. In our marriage, there likely is not. Our wives aren't the enemy and (typically) aren't the existential threat to us that the situation makes them appear to be at first glance. They likely share many of the same principles, morals, and standards that we do. So pause, take a breath, and figure out if this is a DEFCON-level attack situation or if this is something you can sleep on.

Having said all of that, if the remote doesn't get put back, all bets are off. It's an all-call to man battle stations (If you can't tell, we have a problem with TV remotes in our house).

Active Listening – Actually Hearing Them: We've covered this pretty extensively already. I won't rehash the specifics, but we need to understand that, as men, we must do a better job of fully focusing on what our wives are saying instead of planning our hardware store shopping list in our heads while they're talking. We get bonus points if we nod and say "Tell me more" at the right moments.

Social Skills – Communication Superpowers: As discussed, good social skills mean you can express yourself clearly and handle disagreements without turning them into World War III. It's about teamwork, not trying to "win" every argument.

Adaptability – Rolling with the Punches: Marriage isn't static. Being adaptable means going with the flow when life throws curveballs – like when your romantic weekend getaway turns into a DIY plumbing adventure because the sink exploded.

What's more, humans aren't static. They are constantly growing and changing. If you think this concept doesn't especially apply to women...well, this book is probably a little too advanced for you, and we need to back up and start with some more foundational concepts. The point is, it's all good. If you're like me, you have to stop getting so wrapped around the axle when your wife changes her mind or her position on a certain topic. Things change. Cool. You can fight it, but you'll just die tired... and on the couch.

Patience – The Virtue You Didn't Know You'd Need So Much: Patience is key when your wife takes forever to pick a Netflix show or can't decide what color wall paint she wants (aren't they both gray?). It also plays a pivotal role when the "Can I ask you a question?" turns into a 20-minute background diatribe with no indication that a question is on the horizon. It's about staying calm instead of letting minor frustrations snowball into a problem you don't need in your life.

Gratitude – Focusing on the Good Stuff: Gratitude appreciates the little things your wife does, like making your eggs with just the right amount of cheese, supporting your latest obsession with backyard beekeeping, or tolerating your new "mustache phase" that makes you look like a pedophile. Gratitude is also loving the quirks about your wife that everyone else (including you, at times) finds annoying. True, deep, and abiding love allows us to turn those quirks into irresistible charms that we wouldn't trade for the world. Pro tip: Don't use this argument to excuse your wretched farts. That boat don't float.

Humor - The Glue That Keeps You Laughing Together: It might be hard to tell, but I'm a sucker for a good sense of humor. There is nothing I find funnier than laughing at (not with) myself. I'm blessed to have a wife who is able to introspectively laugh at us (me) as well. A good sense of humor can lighten the mood, ease tension, and make even the toughest moments more bearable. Plus, laughing together creates a deeper bond.

When practiced regularly, these aspects of emotional intelligence can help make your marriage not just functional but fun, loving, and resilient. After all, the key to a great relationship isn't perfection – it's navigating imperfections together.

Exercises to Build EI

Empathy Mapping: Imagine a situation from her perspective. What might she be feeling, thinking, or worried about?

Shared Goals: Sit down together and create a vision for your marriage. This is a powerful way to connect emotionally.

Jenny's Comments

Meb has packed a ton into one chapter. I think communication (lack of or abundance of) can make or break any relationship. No communication (ignoring each other) just sucks and creates a mountain of hurt feelings. Bad communication (fighting, name-calling, throwing verbal punches, rehashing the same arguments, bringing up old hurts) creates fissures that take eons to mend. We can't take back words once they've been said, but with good communication, you can create positive experiences and memories that can replace those painful moments.

I like Meb's examples and practical exercises of active listening and emotional intelligence. My eyes and ears notice everything. So does my intuition and keen "Spidey senses". I create an entire narrative in my own mind that is true to me (pay attention to what I just said there because it's all about how we PERCEIVE a thing vs. what is intended) based on what his body is saying vs. what words are coming out of his mouth. If my feelings are hurt by his body language and facial expressions (sighs, eye rolls, foot tapping, voice inflection, speed talking), then that is my perception and experience through our communication...leaving it a negative interaction. Now, I can take whatever words he has chosen to use, and they can be received as negative (even if not intended that way). I walk away, deflated and exhausted. The reality, to him, is that he has a ton on his mind, the weight of the world on his shoulders, and he needs me to have grace and be patient.

I have a lot of work to do in this department. For years (this even still rears its ugly head now and then), my go-to move was to just shut down. It was way easier than putting up a fight. I'd been married to the military for decades. I'd gotten very used to being 2nd place. Maybe even 3rd, 4th, or 5th place for the duration of his military career. I was usually "the most wrong" in any argument, and instead of making the problem worse, I would shut down and finish all arguments in my own head, all alone. Now that he actually WANTS to talk to me and tries to get me to open up, I (embarrassingly) don't even know what to say a lot of the time and need to take a moment or two to gather my thoughts. Meb has changed so much since retirement and has continued to change as we have embraced faith, religion, and spirituality into our lives, and now he approaches me with humility and collaboration rather than contempt and disregard-making me feel human and safe.

I want to address a point that Meb made earlier in the chapter. He spoke about having patience during the 20-minute "Can I ask you a question?" This is playing out even worse for us right now. I got very sick over the last year. I was in and out of surgeries, hospital stays, and emergency room visits. I came dangerously close, many times, to not pulling through. The physical trauma has created neurological damage. I now lose words and have gaps in speech. My response time is laden with mental pauses and frustration over lost vocabulary. My now 20-minute responses have turned into 40-minute responses, or just "giving up" and wanting to spare the poor man the time it's about to take for me to explain how lunch with my girlfriends went or how a work project is shaping up. His patience has tripled since

I've recovered from being so sick. He now lovingly waits for all responses and tries his hardest NOT to show impatience while I work through a difficult sentence. I can't tell you how much that means to me.

Final Thoughts

Improving communication doesn't happen overnight. It's a journey – and yes, you're going to mess up along the way. But the good news is that every small step you take brings you closer to a deeper connection with your wife.

CHAPTER 2

LET'S GET READY TO RUMBLE!

MANAGING STRESS AND CONFLICT CONSTRUCTIVELY

S tress is like that unwelcome houseguest who shows up uninvited, overstays their welcome, and leaves a mess behind. It creeps into your marriage, often disguised as a bad day at work, a pile of bills, or a toddler who refuses to eat anything that isn't shaped like a dinosaur. And when stress isn't managed well, it turns minor disagreements into full-blown arguments.

The good news? Conflict doesn't have to be destructive. In fact, handling it the right way can actually strengthen your marriage. Think of it as sandpaper – it's rough, but it can smooth things out in the end. The key is learning how to manage stress and navigate disagreements with grace, patience, and (maybe) even a little humor.

Mindfulness Practices for Stress Relief

Before we discuss conflict resolution, let's talk about stress. If you're constantly on edge, snapping at your wife because you hit every red light on your way home, it's time to learn some stress management techniques.

What Is Mindfulness?

Mindfulness isn't about sitting cross-legged on a mountaintop chanting "om." It's about being fully present in the moment without judgment. Think of it as hitting the pause button on your racing thoughts.

Practical Mindfulness Techniques

Breathing Exercises: When you're feeling overwhelmed, take a deep breath in for four seconds, hold it for four seconds, and exhale for four seconds. Hold the exhale for four seconds. Repeat until you feel calmer. This is called the Box Breathing technique.

Body Scan Meditation: Close your eyes and focus on each part of your body, starting at your toes and working your way up. This helps you release tension you didn't even realize you were holding.

Mindful Breaks: Step away from your desk or put down your phone and spend five minutes focusing on your surroundings. Notice the colors, sounds, and smells around you.

Mindfulness as a Couple

Practicing mindfulness together can be a game-changer. The following techniques will seem {{ahem}} "interesting" to the uninitiated, but if you spend a lot of time letting stress impact your marriage, what have you got to lose? If taken seriously, these techniques might promote mindfulness while fostering connection and intimacy, helping you strengthen your bond in the present moment:

Mindful Walks: Take a walk without distractions. Talk about what you notice – trees, clouds, the way the air smells.

Guided Meditation: Use an app to do a short meditation together before bed.

Practice Gratitude Together: Take turns sharing one thing you're grateful for each day. This simple practice shifts focus from stress to appreciation and fosters a deeper connection.

Cook a Meal Together Mindfully: Turn cooking into a shared mindfulness practice by focusing on the process – chopping, stirring, and tasting – without rushing. Engage all your senses and enjoy the experience of creating something together.

Body Scan Meditation: Like a similar individual technique, you can do this as a couple. Lie down together and do a guided body scan, focusing on each part of your body and releasing tension. This can help you both relax and become more aware of your physical and emotional state.

Create a Couple's Vision Board: Spend an afternoon cutting out images or writing down goals that reflect your shared dreams and values. This activity promotes intentional conversations about your future and deepens connection.

Silent Eye Contact: Spend a few minutes sitting face-to-face and looking into each other's eyes without speaking. Although this technique can initially feel vulnerable, it often leads to a deep sense of connection, presence, and intimacy. If done incorrectly, it can also be a great way to inject humor into the relationship!

Create a Daily Ritual: Start or end the day with a mindful ritual, such as having herbal tea together, journaling side by side, or simply holding hands and reflecting on the day. A consistent practice grounds your relationship in being present.

Reflect on a Positive Memory: Take a moment to recall a happy memory you share and talk about it in detail. This practice shifts your focus to positivity and strengthens your emotional bond.

UNDERSTANDING AND MANAGING **Triggers**

Ever find yourself snapping over something trivial, like – oh, I don't know – a misplaced remote, and wondering why you're so angry? Chances are, it wasn't about the remote – it was about a deeper trigger. Identifying and managing your triggers is crucial for healthy conflict resolution (but seriously, maybe it was just about the remote...).

How to Identify Your Triggers

Start by reflecting on recent arguments. What really set you off? Common triggers include:

- Feeling disrespected or unappreciated.
- Financial stress.
- Being interrupted.
- Being ignored.

Keep a journal of your reactions. Over time, patterns will emerge, helping you recognize what's really bothering you.

Communicating Triggers to Your Wife

Once you've identified your triggers, talk to your wife about them. Use "I feel," "I perceive," or "I" statements to keep things constructive:

- "I feel overwhelmed when we talk about money without a plan in place."
- "When I'm interrupted, I perceive it to mean that no one cares about what I'm saying."

- "I get frustrated when I feel like my efforts around the house aren't noticed."

This isn't about blaming her – it's about helping her understand your perspective.

Having Difficult Conversations

If the thought of having a tough conversation with your wife makes you break out in a cold sweat, you're not alone. The thought gives me "nervous tummy" just as I sit here typing this. But here's the thing: avoiding these types of talks doesn't make the problem go away. It just lets it fester until someone (probably you) explodes. You then find yourself in the awkward position of trying to defend why you just yelled at the dog because you can't find the TV remote.

It's important to understand that conflict isn't the enemy. In fact, it can be an opportunity to better understand each other and grow as a couple. The trick is learning to fight fair.

The 3 Rules of Engagement

1. *Stay Respectful:* No name-calling, yelling, or dragging up past mistakes. Stick to the issue at hand.

2. *Take Turns Speaking:* Let each person share their perspective without interruptions. Use the active listening techniques we

talked about in Chapter 1 to make sure you understand her perspective.

3. Focus on Solutions: Instead of rehashing the problem, ask, "What can we do to fix this?"

Conflict Resolution – Fighting Fair: Disagreements are inevitable, but how you handle them matters. As stated above, it's about addressing the issue without dragging in the time she gave you a b.s. anniversary gift six years ago.

Typically, I am not a proponent of the "fighting fair" concept. Maybe it's my military background, but my opinion usually is that a fair fight just means that you didn't come to the battle properly prepared. If it's worth fighting over, it's worth doing what you need to do (fair or not) to win. But I've learned from a BUNCH of trial-and-error that this mindset doesn't apply to marriage.

You WILL fight in your marriage. My experience has shown there will inevitably be some conflicts that will reach Old Testament biblical proportions. I have come to understand that some of the greatest growth our marriage has experienced has come from some of these "refining moments." How you handle these moments will be what determines if you are together or apart afterward. The "winner take all" approach to conflict will eventually end up in divorce. The "us against the world" approach to conflict will use conflict to strengthen bonds to an unbreakable level.

THE ART of Timing

Timing is everything. Don't try to discuss the budget five minutes before bed or hash out parenting strategies in the middle of a toddler tantrum. Find a quiet moment when you're both calm and focused. Pro tip: a walk or a "drive to nowhere" can do wonders for setting the tone.

Techniques for Constructive Conflict

The Soft Start-Up: Instead of diving in with an agenda or accusations, start with something gentle, like, "Hey, can we talk about something that's been on my mind?" This is a very delicate phase in a difficult conversation. It is important that in this "rapport" phase, you don't jump headlong into the address to Congress that's been stewing in your mind for the last three days. I'll put it this way: the _second_ that your approach is perceived as an attack is the very moment that defenses will go up – something that makes your job infinitely worse. And listen to me here: _it doesn't matter_ if you meant for it to be an attack or not. It _only_ matters how she perceives it. So, spend a bit of time asking about her stressors _and listening._ Then, gently ease into your issue.

Put Her on Your Side of the Table: Once someone explained this concept to me in a way that resonated, I was blown away by its simplicity and effectiveness. Admittedly, I only get it right about 30% of the time, but when I do...look out! The concept is pretty simple: Find a way to make the issue your enemy instead of her. Present the issue in a way that lets her know that you are genuine in coming up with a _joint_ solution to the problem. So, for example, instead of saying something like, "You haven't had sex with me in two weeks!" (a sure-fire way to make sure that the streak goes on for another two weeks), you might want to try something like, "Lately, I've been feeling like our marriage has lost a bit of the intimacy that is so important to us. Do you think we could come up with some ideas to bring that back?" Welcome to the Jedi-level of difficult conversations.

The Win-Win Mindset: Remember, the goal isn't to win the argument – it's to find a solution you both feel good about. You're a strategic guy. You're smart. So concentrate on the long game and keep your eye on the prize. By the end of the conversation, you want your wife to be more in love with you than she is right now… *and* you want the conflict resolved. Let me say it a different way: the loneliest, most hollow victory in the world is when I am sleeping on the couch after proving that I was right in an argument. There's no one to celebrate the victory with, especially not my best friend.

And that's the point. If I won, that meant that she lost. I don't know about you, but I didn't marry a loser. I certainly don't want to be the reason that she feels like one. So why would I want to put her in that category? On the other hand, I have a private, gleeful satisfaction when I can maneuver a difficult conversation so deftly that it ends with a hug and an agreement (on both our parts) to do better. The bonus is that 100% of the time that I'm able to do this, I've learned something new about my wife. And that's pretty awesome.

It's Not About Coming to an Agreement: This is a key concept to get down, and you *will* struggle with it initially. Very rarely is a difficult discussion ended with one party changing their mind and agreeing on the other's stance. It is important to grasp that it's not about agreeing. You *don't have to agree with your wife, and she doesn't have to agree with you* (we should probably take a respectful moment to pause and allow that truth bomb to finish exploding). The truth is, on contentious topics, I rarely agree with Jenny. What's more, I cannot think of a time during a difficult conversation that I have crafted my argument so successfully that Jenny has turned to me and said, "You know what, Meb? You've convinced me. You're so smart. Your way is much better than my way." (I mean, she's said it 100x in my head, but never out loud. I'm *sure* she's always thinking it!)

The point here is that it is not about agreeing. _It's about understanding._ What is her stance on this topic? Why is she passionate enough about it to make it a heated conversation? Are there underlying issues for her? What has happened in her life that has helped shape or inform this opinion? The questions go on. When I start diving deep into understanding the answers to these questions, I often start to see the other side of the coin. And perspective is never a bad thing. When I am really on my game and can approach a difficult conversation with the goal of understanding (rather than agreeing), I end up learning so much more about how amazing my wife is!

Tools for Diffusing Tension

When things get heated, some things you might try:

Take a Break: Pause the conversation and agree to revisit it later. There is an art to this. In the heat of the moment, simply walking away or saying, "That's it, I need a break," will likely not help anything and might even make things even worse. Instead, you must craft your need for a break in a message that doesn't pour fuel on the flames. Something like, "This conversation seems to be getting heated, at least on my end. I don't want this to turn into a big argument. Can we take a break and come back to this in ten minutes?"

Notice the end of that phrasing. Nothing is worse than "taking a break" that turns into a week's worth of the silent treatment where you are just co-existing under the same roof and walking on eggshells, trying not to make the situation worse. It's okay to take breaks to de-escalate the tension, but don't leave the discussion without a specific time to reengage.

Easier said than done, right? I hear ya'. Frankly, in some conversations (let's stop sugarcoating it and just call them arguments), it is too far past my mental and emotional capacity to make sure my phrasing, tone, and body language are all dialed in perfectly. So sometimes it's helpful to have a "break codeword".

I remember when Jenny and I were going through a very hard time in our marriage. We were having extremely difficult conversations daily, often several times a day. Our counselor told us to take breaks to keep things at a manageable level. During one of the "calms before the storm," we set up a codeword that we could use that meant, "Let's stop this conversation, take a break for 10 minutes, and then come back and reengage with the goal of coming to an understanding." There were times when those 10 minutes just calmed us down enough to politely ask (with the right words, tone, and body language) for another 10 minutes. But that's ok. I can't tell you how helpful it was for both of us to 1) see that this was important enough to the other person that they wanted to use tools to keep the situation from getting worse and 2) know that the issue wasn't going to be left unresolved indefinitely.

A final word of caution on taking breaks. It is counterproductive to use your break to wind yourself up further and reengage in a more negative manner. This break is NOT the time to be bolstering your argument, stewing on some perceived insult, or obsessing over, "I shoulda' said ______." Both of you must agree that the break is to calm down, gain perspective, or seek understanding. Heck, sometimes the break is just to do some deep breathing exercises while you think about puppies.

Use Humor: Humor is like the WD-40 of relationships – it can loosen up even the stickiest situations. A well-timed joke or a playful comment can diffuse tension and remind you both not to take things too seriously. A light-hearted comment can break the tension. A few rules when it comes to humor:

Be Playful, Not Sarcastic: There's a fine line between humor and snark. Keep it lighthearted and kind.

Acknowledge the Absurd: Sometimes, the things we argue about are downright silly. Laughing at the absurdity can help you both see the bigger picture.

As guys, we need practical examples, so hopefully this helps:

Bad examples of humor in a difficult conversation:

"Is it the blonde you got put in your hair last week that is keeping you from understanding my point?"

"While you're on that ten-minute break, would you mind making me a sandwich?"

Good examples of humor in a difficult conversation:

"I'm not a complete idiot – some idiot parts are missing."

"Stop trying to make everyone happy. You're not a taco."

"Every time you start to get angry, I suddenly have the "nervous poops." I wish your anger affected me in different ways (wink, wink)!" (Just a small public service announcement here: while sex jokes in the heat of an argument may ease some of the tension, they will likely not get you laid. So, manage expectations appropriately. You're welcome.)

Another pro tip is to use some word that is funny to both of you as your "take a break codeword." Nothing eases tension more and sets the stage for a good 10-minute break than to yell, "Pumpernickel!" before storming off. You can't even say the word in a genuinely angry manner. Try it. I dare you.

A final word of caution on the use of humor: timing and a shared sense of what is funny are important here. You don't want to be perceived as not taking the conversation seriously. For example, Jenny hates my Dad Jokes. No, that's not quite accurate. Jenny _loathes_ my Dad Jokes. I have perfected the art of weaponizing Dad Jokes to the point that the CIA is now using them in place of waterboarding. In the heat of the moment, I have found it NOT helpful to say something like, "You know honey, I'm sorry. I'm probably not thinking clearly because I was up all night wondering where the sun went...and then it dawned on me!" Let's just say that – for some reason that I will never understand – this use of humor has never been appreciated.

Developing a Conflict Resolution Framework

Every couple needs a game plan for handling disagreements. Think of it as a roadmap that keeps you both on track, even when emotions run high.

Step-by-Step Conflict Resolution

1. Identify the Issue: Be specific. Instead of saying, "You never help around the house," say, "I need more help with the dishes."

2. Share Perspectives: Take turns explaining your point of view without interruptions.

3. Brainstorm Solutions: Collaborate to generate ideas. The goal is to find a win-win solution, not a win-lose one.

4. Agree on a Plan: Choose a solution and decide how you'll implement it.

A Word-or-Two About the Man's Role in Creating Safe Spaces

As a husband, one of your most crucial roles is to create a *safe space* where both you and your wife feel heard, respected, and valued – even in the heat of an argument. A safe space doesn't mean avoiding conflict; it means fostering an environment where both of you can express emotions and perspectives without fear of being dismissed, belittled, or attacked.

Like it or not, men have a greater responsibility to be mindful of the perception of danger and safety when arguing. A heated tone, a profane word, misuse of sarcasm, a clenched fist, or a jerked movement coming from an angry man can send an unintended message of danger that can completely derail conflict resolution efforts. Keep this in mind. As angry as you may get, you can make it infinitely worse if you are not mindful of your verbal and non-verbal signals – intended or not. _It is more your responsibility than hers_ to set a tone of safety and security in an argument.

Start by leading with calmness and empathy, even when the conversation gets tough. Listen actively – focus on what she's saying instead of formulating your counterargument. Avoid interrupting or raising your voice; instead, validate her feelings with phrases like, "I see why you feel that way" or "That makes sense." Show that you value her thoughts, even if you disagree. Avoid blame or harsh criticism, and resist the urge to "win" the argument. Instead, aim to understand her point of view and work toward resolution as a team.

Your nonverbal cues also matter. Crossing your arms, rolling your eyes, or displaying frustration can escalate the conflict. Instead, maintain open body language and keep your tone steady. By staying grounded, you model emotional regulation and set the tone for productive conversations. Creating a safe space for arguments is ultimately about showing your wife that your love and respect for her outweigh any temporary disagreement. It's a way of saying, "I'm here for us, no matter what."

When to Seek Help

Some conflicts are bigger than what you can handle on your own. If you're stuck in a cycle of fighting without resolution, or if it's an issue that needs a professional, consider seeking help from a counselor or therapist. There's no shame in getting professional guidance – it's an investment in your relationship. Sometimes, it is literally "just what the doctor ordered" to get you unstuck. Jenny and I owe a huge debt of gratitude to the therapists and counselors in our personal lives and in our marriage who have helped us learn how to fight _for_ our marriage and not _with_ our marriage.

Jenny's Comments

I hate to argue. My heart rate increases, my face gets hot, my head starts to hurt, and my tummy goes gang-busters. Arguments turn into anxiety for me. I spoke a little bit in the last chapter about the health challenges that I had over the last year. It was all due to GI issues being completely jacked up. Knowing this, Meb has chosen to take my anxiety and make it his goal in life to protect me from getting anxious or stressed out. He desperately tries to keep me calm because an anxiety trigger can have me down for the count for days as I wrestle with getting my GI issues back under control.

With this in mind, he has truly tried to change the way we tackle disagreements. He tries not to "fight" with me. We are not perfect in this area, but we are a heck of a lot different than we were in our first 30 years of marriage.

Unfortunately, neither Meb nor I had good role models as our parents. We did not learn what a healthy marriage looks like by watching their examples. My single mother was never in a relationship during my entire childhood, and she did not speak highly of my father (whom I barely know and do not have close contact with). Meb's parents were dismissive of each other and their three boys, leaving Meb to figure things out on his own.

I do have to admit that when we get into knockdown, drag-out fights (literally, not figuratively), we go for the jugular—at least we used to. It's been quite a while since one of these has occurred, as we have tried to implement many changes into our lives, one of which is prayer.

There's something about praying for our spouse and our marriage (specifically during a heated argument) that humbles us, slows things down, and puts it all into perspective. This is a new practice for us both, and boy, has it taken things to an entirely different level. Using prayer during a "fight," for me, has helped me not to see Meb as the spawn of Satan but as an imperfect man who is just trying his best and trying to give me his best. That has helped me to offer grace and apply forgiveness to our marriage. "I'm sorry" means so much to me. "I was wrong" is also something I need to hear. I have a choice to make when Meb offers those words to me. I can use it against him and continue the battle royale (Ding-Ding!), or I can calm down, take a breath, get perspective, give him the benefit of the doubt, believe him, and sense his urgency to diffuse the situation.

Final Thoughts

Stress and conflict are inevitable, but they don't have to define your marriage. With mindfulness, patience, and a solid conflict resolution plan, you can turn even the toughest disagreements into opportunities for growth.

CHAPTER 3

"SHE ALREADY KNOWS I'M THANKFUL" – NOT!

FOSTERING APPRECIATION AND GRATITUDE

Let's face it: in the hustle and bustle of everyday life, it's easy to take each other for granted. The laundry gets done, the lunches get packed, the bills get paid, and trash cans magically show up on the curb... but how often do you stop and say, "Hey, I appreciate you for doing all of this"?

Gratitude is the secret weapon of happy marriages. It's like the oil that keeps the engine running smoothly. And the best part?

It doesn't take much effort to create a massive shift in your relationship. When you and your wife feel seen, valued, and appreciated, everything else becomes a little easier.

The Gratitude Ritual: Building Positivity

If you think a gratitude practice sounds like something out of a self-help book, you're right – but don't knock it until you try it. Gratitude is scientifically proven to boost happiness, reduce stress, and strengthen relationships. Plus, it's a lot less ridiculous than some things that are "scientifically proven." (For example, did you know that it is scientifically proven that goats have accents? Seriously. Look it up.)

Morning Gratitude

Start each day by reflecting on one thing you appreciate about your wife. It could be something big ("I love how you always support my dreams") or something small ("Thanks for feeding the dogs this morning; I was running late."). Share it with her, or just keep it in mind to set a positive tone for the day. I take that back. Share it with her. A wife's job is tough enough as it is without withholding anything that could help – even just a little bit.

Other Gratitude-Sharing Ideas

Before bed, take turns sharing three things you were grateful for that day. This simple ritual does wonders for shifting your focus from what went wrong to what went right. If you're the journaling type, keep a notebook by your bed and jot down one thing you're grateful for about your wife each night. Bonus points if you share these entries with her occasionally – it's like a handwritten love letter, one day at a time.

Recognizing and Celebrating Small Wins

Big anniversaries and grand gestures are great, but the magic of marriage is often found in the small wins. Did she handle a stressful situation like a pro? Did you both survive the week without arguing over the thermostat? Celebrate it!

Everyday Celebrations

Write a Note: Leave a sticky note that says, "Thanks for being amazing today."

High-Five Your Wins: Yes, literally. When you accomplish something as a team (like fixing the sink or surviving a PTA meeting), give her a high-five and make it fun.

Acknowledge the Little Things: "Thanks for folding my shirts the way I like them," for example, goes a long way toward making her feel appreciated.

Weekly Recaps

Make it a habit to reflect on the week together. Ask, "What's one thing you're proud of this week?" It's a great way to acknowledge efforts and celebrate accomplishments.

The Language of Appreciation: Making Your Spouse Feel Valued

Saying "thank you" is nice, but it's just the beginning. True appreciation comes from understanding what makes your wife feel valued and expressing it in a way that resonates with her.

Speak Her Language

If you haven't explored Chapman's concept of love languages yet, now's the time. Here's how they can help:

Words of Affirmation: If this is her love language, verbal appreciation is key. Tell her she's amazing, brilliant, and beautiful – and mean it.

Acts of Service: Show your gratitude by doing something helpful, like making dinner or taking the car for an oil change.

Quality Time: Spend uninterrupted time together, whether it's a date night or just sitting on the couch talking.

Gifts: A small, thoughtful gift can go a long way. It doesn't have to be expensive – a single flower or her favorite chocolate bar will do.

Physical Touch: A hug, a kiss, or a simple hand squeeze can speak volumes.

Be Specific

Generic compliments like "You're great" don't pack much punch. Instead, be specific: "The color of that shirt really makes your eyes pop!" or "I love how you always know the right thing to say when I'm stressed," or "Thanks for organizing the family schedule - it makes life so much easier," or "Thank you for always folding the laundry, it's a thankless job that no one wants, and the chore isn't going anywhere until I can convince you that we should join a nudist colony!"

Creating a Culture of Kindness at Home

Imagine your home as a little bubble of kindness in a chaotic and stressful world – a sanctuary, a Holy Ground. By fostering a culture of kindness, you create an environment where both you and your wife feel supported and appreciated.

Lead by Example

Kindness is contagious. When you go out of your way to be kind, your wife (and even your kids) will naturally follow suit. Start with small acts:

- Offer to help with her to-do list without being asked.
- Compliment her in front of others.
- Leave a treat on her desk or nightstand.

Couple Kindness Challenges

Once you've set the tone, work as a couple to create and implement kindness challenges. These "Kindness Challenge" ideas are simple, fun, and guaranteed to bring more joy and connection into your relationship:

Random Acts of Kindness Day: Jenny likes to call these "RAK Attacks," and she's grown them into a community-wide activity. Dedicate one day a month to surprising each other with kind gestures.

Compliment Bingo: Create a bingo card with specific compliments (e.g., "You're a great cook," "You're hilarious," "You're rocking that outfit") and try to mark off as many as you can in a week. It's like bingo, but instead of shouting "BINGO!" you're basking in the glow of appreciation.

The Gratitude Jar: Keep a jar where you both write down things you're grateful for. At the end of the month, read the entries together.

The Chore Swap Challenge: Switch chores for a week to show kindness and appreciation. If you usually do the dishes and your partner takes out the trash, swap tasks. You might even gain a newfound respect for what the other does (or learn why your partner insists you *rinse before loading*). If you don't usually help with household chores, then your wife is REALLY going to love this challenge!

Surprise Snack Attack: Each partner secretly buys or prepares the other's favorite snack during the week. Whether it's a bag of peanut butter cups or a plate of freshly baked cookies, food equals love – especially when it's unexpected.

Morning Love Note Marathon: For one week, leave a sweet or silly note in a spot your partner will find in the morning (bathroom mirror, car dashboard, coffee machine). Bonus points for creativity or bad puns.

"You Choose" Night: Take turns dedicating one evening a week to doing whatever the other person wants – no complaints allowed. Whether it's watching their favorite guilty-pleasure movie (*yes, even rom-coms*) or eating at their go-to taco joint, it's all about putting their preferences first.

DIY Compliment Coupons: Make a few compliment "coupons" your partner can redeem anytime. Examples: "Redeem for a compliment about your outfit" or "Redeem for me to gush about how great you are." It's quirky, cute, and customizable.

Compliment Ping-Pong: Sit down face-to-face and take turns giving each other compliments, rapid-fire. The first person to run out of things to say loses. Prepare to dig deep – and possibly laugh a lot.

The Laugh Mission: Dedicate one week to making your partner laugh daily. It could be through silly jokes, funny memes, or dramatic reenactments of ridiculous.

Recognizing the Impact of Positive Affirmations

Positive affirmations might sound like motivational poster material, but they're incredibly effective in building confidence and connection.

How to Craft Affirmations

An affirmation is simply a positive statement that reinforces something true or aspirational. For example:

- "I am grateful for the strong partnership we've built together."
- "We are a team, and we can handle anything together."

Sharing Affirmations

Work with your wife to come up with positive affirmations about your marriage. Take turns exchanging with daily. It might feel a little awkward at first, but over time, it becomes a powerful way to stay connected.

Keeping It Fun

Appreciation doesn't have to be serious all the time. Adding a touch of humor and playfulness makes it even more effective. For example:

- "Thanks for not killing me when I forgot our anniversary three years ago. You're the best."
- "I appreciate how you always find my keys when I lose them. You're basically my personal GPS."
- "Thank you for always talking me back off of the edge. Society owes you a deep debt of gratitude for saving them from my wrath."

Jenny's Comments

Wow, Meb! Thanks for writing such a great chapter (see what I did there?)! I recently noticed that Meb makes sure to ask me what I'd like from the fridge, from the garage, or from the basement so that I don't have to get it myself. Then, when he brought it to me, I wasn't really saying anything. Like, what kind of selfish ingrate does that?! So, I've been trying harder to just say "Thank You" for the kind gestures that Meb does for me throughout the day. I absolutely miss the gestures on the days that they aren't offered, so now I hope to acknowledge them more fully when they are.

Also, Meb is a hopeless romantic. He's actually had that in him throughout our entire marriage, it has just manifested in different ways throughout the years. Meb's new thing is to write a few sentences about what he loves about me onto a sticky note. Then, he's been placing the sticky notes on my bathroom mirror, in a heart shape, right around where my reflection stands when I look into the mirror. There are some that are my favorites. My very favorite one says, *"You should be <u>very</u> proud of the way your husband feels about his marriage! I love you!"* What a gift he just gave to me. I don't think that's lip service or trying to get something from me. That's just a heartfelt declaration of love that allows me to have gratitude for HIM!

Final Thoughts

Gratitude and appreciation are like marriage superpowers. They don't just make your wife feel loved – they also remind you of how lucky you are to have her. So start small, stay consistent, and watch how these simple practices transform your relationship.

CHAPTER 4

"HONEY, I'LL BE HOME LATE AGAIN"

ACHIEVING WORK-LIFE BALANCE

Work-life balance. Just hearing the phrase can make you roll your eyes, right? It sounds like one of those buzzwords they throw around in corporate meetings alongside "synergy" and "thinking outside the box." But when you're married, balance isn't optional – it's survival.

If you're constantly working late, bringing work stress home, glued to your phone, or missing another soccer game because of "one last email," it's only a matter of time before it takes a toll on your marriage. The good news? You don't need to quit your job and move to a cabin in the woods to find balance. With a few changes, you can create space for what matters most.

Prioritizing Family Time in a Demanding World

The harsh truth? Your wife and kids don't care how many hours you logged or how big your latest project is. They care that you're *there* – physically, emotionally, and without a Bluetooth headset stuck to your ear. But in a world where work emails ping at all hours and "hustle culture" encourages being perpetually busy, prioritizing family time can feel like swimming against the tide. Here's how to make it happen and why it matters.

The Myth of Quality Over Quantity

Next, let's debunk a popular excuse: "It's not about how much time you spend; it's about the quality of the time." Nice try, but wrong. It's both. Take it from me. I spent 26 years deployed in combat or traveling away from home on training missions. Even when I was stateside, I was constantly working late. I chose hobbies that were solitary in nature, and that kept me outside of the home (cycling, surfing, riding motorcycles, skydiving, etc.). Yet I justified it all by thinking that – when I was with my family – I was going to be the best dad and husband on the planet. I was going to make sure we went to Disneyland, carnivals, movie premiers, etc. That all went over like a turd in a punch bowl. You can't just show up for 15 minutes a week and expect to win Husband of the Year. The brutal truth was that my wife didn't know me. I was a stranger to my daughter. And I didn't know them either. It made for some awkward and unsuccessful moments as I tried to force the Normal Rockwell family I had as a vision in my head.

I remember showing up at one of my daughter's soccer games. Trying to make up for lost time and appear as the "Super-Dad," I decided it would be a good idea to storm the field and berate our coach, who I felt was being overly critical of my daughter. Of course, I took it WAY overboard and ended up scaring the coach, the parents, the other kids, and – most damagingly – my wife and daughter. There were some other issues at play here, but I can't ignore the fact that my subconscious guided my actions to try and make up for the Father/Husband I knew I was failing to be due to my near-constant absence.

It took me way too long to realize that real connection happens in mundane moments, such as dinner conversations, movie nights, and bedtime stories. Quality _and_ quantity are both critically important, no more so than in a marriage.

Creating Space for Family

Here are some strategies to carve out more family time without quitting your job or cloning yourself:

Schedule It: Put family time on your calendar like you would a meeting. Block off a couple of evenings a week or a weekend afternoon. Treat it as sacred.

Protect It: If someone tries to steal that time – whether it's a client, your boss, or your fishing buddy – learn to say no (more on that later).

Be Fully Present: Turn off your phone, shut the laptop, and show up for your family. No scrolling during game night!

The Dinner Table Rule

There's something magical about sharing a meal. Whether it's a quick Tuesday taco night or a fancy Friday steak dinner, make it a priority (I'm trying to implement "Pizza Oven Sunday," but Jenny keeps telling me it's not a "thing"...we'll see!). Research shows families who eat together communicate better, argue less, and laugh more. Bonus: you might even learn something about your kids beyond, "Nothing happened at school today."

I gotta add a caveat to this one. As I type this, Jenny and I are a semi-retired, empty-nest couple. I realize that we have let the sanctity of dinner time slip. Meals are a lot less formal and more of a "dinner is on the stove whenever you find a break in whatever you have going on." I need to do a better job of resurrecting that precious opportunity for connection and bonding that dinner time affords. It gives me an opportunity to express gratitude verbally, yes, but also non-verbally because I know that one thing Jenny really likes is to watch her family enjoy her cooking.

So, there is a lesson to be learned here. We all have a never-ending pathway to learning and improving to be better husbands...even those of us who write books about it.

Creating Routines That Support Work-Life Harmony

Let's face it – your life is a chaotic mix of deadlines, school drop-offs, and the occasional attempt at self-care. The key to managing it all is creating routines that reduce stress and make time for what matters. What I hate is suggesting a solution that creates more stress simply by the work required to implement the solution. So, I'm not here to tell you that you need to develop charts, graphs, schedules, or anything else. I'm simply asking you to take a look at what you have going on this week and see if there is some open time that you could block off and label "Critical Development Meeting." Later, we'll discuss what specific activities you might want to think about to assist in the development of your marriage.

The Power of a Morning Routine

Ever notice how a stressful morning can derail your entire day? Flip the script with a morning routine that sets the tone for success:

Wake Up Before the Chaos: Even 15 minutes of quiet time can make a huge difference. Use it to pray, stretch, meditate, just sit, or plan your day. Make "me time" a priority, but schedule it at a time of day that doesn't impact the time you have available for your wife and kids.

Start with Gratitude: Take a moment to appreciate what you have. It sounds cheesy, but it works.

I've recently acquired what I term "old man disease." I am exhausted by 9:00 pm, but I am wide awake at 4:30 am. This is early, even for an old Army Sergeant Major! Rather than fight it, I've found that I can capitalize on a whole two hours of "me time" before the house (or the world, for that matter) typically starts their daily routine. I have been able to use this time to do a myriad of "centering" activities that truly make a difference to the start of my day. I feed the dogs, stretch, pray, read my scriptures, and meditate. I'll go over my schedule for the day and make sure my to-do list is locked in (I'm a big to-do list guy). I can tell that it helps because – on the days that my morning routine gets curtailed for whatever reason – Jenny says that I seem more agitated and "moody" (for the record, I don't get moody!).

Bedtime Rituals for Connection

Bedtime isn't just for kids – it's for couples, too. Instead of scrolling your phones until one of you passes out, try this:

Talk about your day: Share one good thing and one challenge.

Turn off the TV for thirty minutes: The only rule for that time is that you have to be touching each other. That could be a hand on the knee, a head on the lap, a back rub, or something a little more...adventurous. You can talk, listen to music, sit in silence, or read something (a book, a devotional, an article, whatever), but the focus is on connection, not whatever the activity is.

Pray as a couple: Bonding together with gratitude or pleas for help sends a powerful message to the adversary that this is a unified coalition working with the Creator for help and protection.

Routines like these build connection and ensure you end the day on the same page. Admittedly, I have varying success establishing consistency with this routine. I have gone through phases where I will read a chapter of a book every night to Jenny while she takes a bath. Sometimes, these were marriage help books, sometimes they were religious books, and sometimes they were whatever novel she was currently working her way through. The book really didn't matter to me (nor do I think to her). What did matter was the quality time.

Setting Boundaries: Protecting Your Family Space

Your family needs boundaries to thrive. Without them, work creeps into every corner of your life until you're answering emails at the dinner table and taking calls during soccer games. Here are some strategies to help set those boundaries.

Design Work-Free Zones: Pick a few places in your home that are completely off-limits for work, such as the dining room, the living room, or maybe even your bedroom. Yes, that may mean no laptops in bed.

The Art of Saying No: This one's tough, especially if you're used to saying yes to everything. But here's the deal: every time you say yes to something, you're saying no to something else. Is that late-night work call worth missing bedtime stories? Probably not. There are times that – as the family provider – you have no choice. But you must objectively assess every situation on its own merit. If you find that you are saying "yes" to work (and therefore "no" to family) more often than not, then you must consider the message you are sending to your family and the long-term impact this will have on your family relationships. Here are some helpful suggestions to make this a bit easier:

Practice saying no gracefully: Develop some pat statements so you don't have to think of them in the moment, such as "Thanks for thinking of me, but I have family commitments." or "I'd love to help, but I'm not available right now."

This is something I wish I would have learned a lot earlier in my career. I was a constant over-achiever and go-getter. I was always looking to be promoted quicker than my peers and needed to show that I could be more dedicated and take on more responsibility than everyone else. My dad had instilled a very healthy work ethic in all of us boys, and I took pride in showing that I could outwork anyone in the room. Add on top of this that it was a military career, where the opportunities to say "no" were somewhat limited. It was a recipe for disaster.

This had a tremendously negative impact on my relationship with my daughter and truly sent a horrible message to my wife. Years of living this lifestyle conditioned my family to believe that they were not the highest priority in my life. If I'm being honest with myself, they weren't. Brutal truth will tell me that there were many opportunities where I could have made my fatherhood and my marriage a priority, but I consistently made choices that prioritized my career under the guise of "providing a better life for my family." Ironically, this led to disastrous consequences that did the exact opposite. It was only after I retired that I was ready to turn to my family and prioritize those relationships. The only problem was that, by that time, my wife and daughter had been conditioned for over two decades to "do without" and had developed coping skills to live a life that did not include me. Recovering from this took a lot of hard work. It shocked my wife the first time I declined a job opportunity in deference for a previously scheduled family outing. I had to pick her up off the floor after I asked her if she wanted to go into business with me. Our marriage now is stronger than I ever imagined it could be and, frankly, better than I deserve. But one of our lingering issues is dealing with some of the emotional scars that come with me prioritizing everything but my family for so long.

So, take it from a guy who loves to give "do what I say, not what I do" advice. Cherish your wife and children. Anytime possible, show them by your actions that they hold the highest priority in your life. I sure wish I had done a better job on this one.

The Art of Meaningful Family Time:

Not all family time is created equal. Watching TV together while you're glued to your phone doesn't count. True connection comes from intentional, engaging activities. Ideas for quality time (wife or family) could include:

Game Nights: Dust off Monopoly or try a new card game. Just be prepared – your wife might be secretly ruthless at Uno.

Here, again, I have to tell on myself. Game Night is one of Jenny's super love languages. Especially those types of games that are fast-paced and require quick thinking and good hand-eye coordination. I can't stand these types of games. I'm more of a fan of games like Risk, Monopoly, or Chess. I like games that are slow, strategic, and can go on for days. The types of games that I like do not typically lend themselves to a "routine" family connection, especially when you are as cutthroat about winning as I am. I'm not saying that I am competitive, but the running joke in our house is that when we play Monopoly, I have to be an all-time banker, and I am the only one who holds all my money in my hand while we play.

BUT – I know this is important to Jenny. Our daughter has inherited her mother's love of fast-paced games that require quick thinking and hand-eye coordination. So, every once in a while (much too rarely for Jenny's liking), I prioritize time with my family, lock away my manic need to dominate at any competition, and just enjoy laughing and spending time doing something my ladies love to do. It's usually worth it. At the very least, it allows them both the opportunity to make fun of how much I suck at those types of games.

Outdoor Adventures: Go for a hike, have a picnic, or just walk around the neighborhood. The great outdoors is magical, even if it means literally getting out of your front door. A 15-minute nightly walk with your spouse after dinner can become a sacred  space to reconnect and unwind together. Some of my most cherished memories are quiet walks in the forest of the Pacific Northwest, sitting on jetties wave-watching in Monterey, or contemplative beach walks with Jenny in La Jolla.

Create Together: Whether it's cooking dinner, growing a garden, or making crafts, creating something as a couple builds memories. As with many marital lessons, I learned this one a little later in life than I would have liked. I absolutely love designing, building, and creating with Jenny. We have done so many joint projects together now. When I look at them, I see US more than I see the project itself. We take mutual pride in the outcome, the work required to achieve it, and (most significantly) the time spent together accomplishing it.

Service: Few things will bring a family –especially a couple – closer than performing some selfless service for someone else. This is a valuable life lesson that I have been honored to learn from Jenny. Jenny has always had a servant's heart. From the early days of our marriage, she has always had a knack for finding and filling a need. For many years, that was just "her thing" that I humored and tolerated. I considered the service I was performing as a military member to be "enough." Boy, was I missing out!

When I finally started to not just tolerate but actively participate in the service projects that Jenny was involved in, I began to see the magic of service and the strength it brought to us as a couple. Together, we've accomplished some pretty amazing things for others. We have volunteered countless hours, efforts, and money to causes and people important to us as a couple. It has strengthened us beyond belief. I'm not ashamed to admit that I am proud to be known as a couple who does service projects together. It's pretty dang cool and is one of the things that truly helps define our marriage.

Addressing the 10 Work-Life Balance Myths

Work-life balance is such an important topic with such a significant impact on marriages that it is important to address some of the myths commonly associated with the concept. If believed, these myths can create unnecessary pressure and misaligned expectations. Busting them allows couples to focus on what truly matters: connection, communication, and a willingness to navigate the ups and downs of life *together*.

Myth #1 – Balance Means 50/50: Balance doesn't mean spending exactly half your time on work and half on family. Some weeks will be work-heavy; others will lean toward family. The key is to stay aware and adjust as needed.

Myth #2 – Multitasking Works: Spoiler alert: multitasking is a lie. It simply isn't applicable when it comes to family and marriages. Trying to work and spend time with your family simultaneously just leaves both sides feeling shortchanged.

Myth #3 – You Can "Have It All" at the Same Time: The idea that you can excel at your career, have a perfect marriage, and raise flawless kids *all at once* is not only unrealistic but also exhausting. Something's gotta give – temporarily. Life happens in seasons. What matters is aligning your priorities with your current stage of life.

Myth #4 – Work Should Never Come Home: While it's important to have boundaries, some work stress will spill over.

Instead of shutting your wife out, talk about it briefly, then transition to family time. Ignoring work at home 100% isn't always realistic – it's about *managing* it, not pretending it doesn't exist.

Myth #5 – One Partner Should Handle Work-Life Balance for Both: The idea that one partner should "manage" the balancing act for the relationship – whether it's coordinating schedules or handling all family responsibilities – is unfair. Balance requires teamwork. Otherwise, one person gets burnt out while the other wonders why things feel "off". I have to admit that I have left much of the responsibility for our social calendar and service engagements to Jenny. As I currently consider this, I am putting it on the list of things I need to improve on in my own marriage.

Myth #6 – Couples Should Always Be Together in Their Free Time: While spending time together is important, expecting to spend *all* your free time together isn't realistic or healthy. Both partners need time to pursue personal interests to recharge, which can actually bring fresh energy to the relationship.

Myth #7 – Work-Life Balance Is Static: Balance isn't a "set it and forget it" thing. Life changes – jobs, kids, health, etc. – and so does what balance looks like. A great marriage adapts to these shifts and renegotiates balance as needed. Sticking to a rigid idea of balance can cause unnecessary friction.

Myth #8 – Kids Come First, Always: While kids are obviously a top priority, putting them above your marriage every single time can weaken the relationship. A strong, loving partnership creates a stable foundation for your family. Taking time to nurture your marriage isn't selfish; it's essential.

Myth #9 – You Need Big Gestures to Show You Care: Grand gestures are nice, but the little daily actions – checking in, helping with chores, or sharing a laugh – are what truly strengthen your bond. Even 10 focused minutes of undistracted attention can leave your family feeling loved and appreciated. You don't need a surprise trip to Paris to make your wife feel loved. (Although she probably wouldn't complain.)

Myth #10 – Balance Means Perfection: The belief that you'll achieve a perfectly balanced life where nothing ever feels off is pure fantasy. Real work-life balance is messy and imperfect, and that's okay. What matters is that you and your wife feel supported through the chaos.

Leveraging Technology for Connection

Up to this point, we've treated technology like it was the next COVID plague. But honestly, technology isn't the enemy – it's how it is used. Like any other aspect of our lives, using technology intentionally can foster connection and make shared responsibilities easier to manage, creating more space for quality time in your marriage. Here are ways to use technology to bring you closer:

Shared Calendars: Keep everyone in the loop with family events and activities. On this note – guys, I'm talking to you on this – collectively, we need to be accountable for putting important dates on our own calendar. Don't just think of anniversaries. Any important milestones in your wife's life, goals met, challenges overcame, etc. *And then set reminders for them.* When you get the alert to pop up on your phone, acknowledge your wife's event. This single use of technology will make you look like a super-husband.

Photo Albums: Create shared albums to document family moments.

Group Chats: Start a family group chat for updates, jokes, and memes.

Virtual Date Nights: When life gets busy, schedule a virtual date night if you're apart – watch the same movie, play an online game together, or even cook "together" over video chat. It's a creative way to stay connected, even long-distance.

Couple's Apps: Use apps like Between, Paired, Love Nudge, and Gottman Card Decks to do cool connection activities, share notes, photos, or even relationship goals. These apps are designed for couples and can help you stay connected in fun, meaningful ways.

Shared To-Do Lists: Use apps like Todoist or Google Keep to manage household tasks together. Nothing says "romantic partnership," like successfully remembering to buy toilet paper or schedule the plumber.

Video Messages: Send short video messages throughout the day instead of just texting. Seeing each other's faces adds a personal touch that a quick "hey" doesn't quite capture.

Daily Reminders or Alarms for Sweet Gestures: Set a daily reminder on your phone to send a loving text, plan a surprise, or simply compliment your wife. A little tech nudge can help keep the romance alive.

Play Online Games Together: Whether it's a light-hearted trivia app or a cooperative game, playing together fosters teamwork and shared laughs. Just don't get too competitive in Mario Kart.

Stream Playlists: Create shared music playlists for road trips, date nights, or even household chores. Jamming out to favorite tunes can make everyday activities more fun. If you're like us and your taste in music varies greatly, make sure there is an equal distribution of Hank Williams and Taylor Swift.

Meal-Planning Apps: Apps like Mealime (no "t") or Cozi can make planning and prepping meals together easier and more collaborative. Plus, fewer "What's for dinner?" debates.

Fitness or Wellness Apps: Stay healthy together with apps that track steps, offer couples yoga sessions, or encourage mindfulness practices. Bonus points if you can cheer each other on through the app!

Just remember to unplug regularly. No app can replace a face-to-face connection.

Jenny's Comments

I have to admit, when I saw the title of this chapter, I got a pit in my stomach. I absolutely HATE (and I mean HATE) how much time the military stole from our family. There were many times that we could (and frankly, should) have had time together rather than Meb taking care of "one more task" until the late-night hours or going on "one more trip" outside of the US. Don't get me wrong...we served this nation with great sacrifice and with great humility. It's a call that many cannot or will not answer. We did it willingly and proudly...for far too long. We are living with the regrets and side effects of those missed birthdays, anniversaries, holidays, important life milestones, and opportunities to create a bond as a family. Something I've learned along the way is that you can't get back time. We aren't getting any younger, healthier, or gaining more energy with the older we get. We are using what we have now to gain the traction that we need. But...we've missed so much.

Except...there was a particularly difficult time in our marriage; we were married 17 years at this point, and our relationship was at the edge of disaster. Suddenly, Meb started telling his military unit to find someone else to go on those trips. He started coming home for lunch, and several times a week, we would meet up at a sushi spot by our home. He made an effort to prioritize our marriage and his family to keep us from crumbling and disintegrating into divorce. Now, whenever we eat sushi, we fondly remember the year of "marriage saving sushi dates."

There have been business trips after military life that Meb has been on, where we created habits of connection. For example, Meb read the *Gone With The Wind* series (two huge books!) to me over the phone while on a few business trips. I cherished and looked forward to that connection time every day, and I still think about it fondly-even though it was probably 6-7 years ago that we did that.

I look now at our grown daughter and her husband. They are young, in love, and have the whole world at their disposal. Like us at their age, they wish things would speed up so that they can have "whatever's next," such as a new career after completing the master's degree, a first-time house purchase after interest rates drop, starting a family after saving up enough money to responsibly take care of children, etc. I wish I could urge them to stop and appreciate where they are now...a "smell the roses" type of mentoring-but we were the exact same way at their age, and I'd be a hypocrite to even begin that type of conversation. I truly am sad that we will never get the time back that we lost for so many of those years spent devoting too much time to focus on work.

Final Thoughts

Work-life balance isn't about perfection – it's about progress. Start small. Prioritize your family, set boundaries, and build routines that work for you. Remember, your career might fund your life, but your family *is* your life. Work will always demand your time, and the world will never stop being busy. But at the end of the day, what your family will remember isn't your job title or your bank balance – it's the moments you spent together. Make those moments count. Because no matter how demanding the world gets, the love and laughter shared with your family will always be the most important investment you'll ever make.

CHAPTER 5

WHEN DO WE TALK ABOUT SEX?

REIGNITING INTIMACY AND PASSION

Ready for the understatement of the year? Keeping the spark alive in marriage isn't always easy (duh!). When you first got together, intimacy came effortlessly. You were all about stolen kisses, long conversations, making toes curl, and that electric feeling of new love. Fast forward a few years (or decades), and you're more likely to fist-bump than hold hands.

But here's the thing: intimacy and passion don't have to fade over time. They just need a little attention. Think of your relationship like a campfire – if you don't tend to it, the flames die down. The good news? As long as there are still some embers, it doesn't take much to reignite the fire.

Rediscovering Each Other: Beyond the Daily Routine

Marriage can feel a little...routine. Wake up, go to work, shuffle the kids around, and fall asleep watching Netflix. Somewhere along the way, the excitement of discovering each other got replaced by debates over whose turn it is to take out the trash. All couples run the risk of getting stuck in this rut. Jenny likes to call it "the roommate rut." More accurately, she *dislikes* to call it "the roommate rut". The danger of the roommate rut is that it is a self-licking ice cream cone; couples in it don't feel the passion, and a lack of passion contributes to the couple feeling like roommates.

So what to do?

The Power of Curiosity

When was the last time you asked your wife about her dreams? Her goals? Her favorite childhood memory? You may have made the same mistake I did: thinking that you've been married so long that you already know everything there is to know about your wife. What I failed to realize is that she is human, too (yes, she is 99% superhuman, but there is 1% that is still human!). Humans continue to change, learn, and grow throughout their lives. Once I applied this realization to my marriage, it has been super neat to re-introduce myself to my wife as I stay engaged. It's exciting to discover new things that I never knew about her! Rediscovering each other starts with curiosity. Here are some questions to get you started:

"What's something you've always wanted to try but never have?": This question uncovers hidden dreams or desires that may not have come up before. It's a way to learn more about her sense of adventure or curiosity and opens the door to exploring new experiences together.

"What's one thing you'd like to do together this year?": This question focuses on shared goals and dreams. It's a great way to prioritize your relationship and make intentional plans for the near future, fostering excitement and collaboration.

"What's a memory of us that always makes you smile?": Reflecting on positive memories strengthens emotional intimacy and allows you to revisit the moments that have brought joy to your relationship. It's also an opportunity to see your relationship through her eyes.

"What's a skill or hobby you've always wanted to learn?": This opens the door to her dreams and aspirations and could inspire something you can explore together.

"What's the most surprising thing you've learned about yourself recently?": Encourages self-reflection and lets her share personal growth or discoveries.

"If you could relive one day from our relationship, what would it be?": A beautiful way to revisit cherished memories and learn which moments meant the most to her.

"What's a place you've never been to that you'd love to visit?": Ignites conversations about travel dreams and maybe sparks a future adventure together.

"What's something small I do that makes you feel loved?": A subtle but impactful way to learn how to keep her feeling appreciated and cared for.

"If we wrote a book about our life together, what would the title be?": (Excuse the irony) This playful question lets her reflect on your journey as a couple with humor or sentimentality.

"What's a habit or tradition you'd love for us to start?": Encourages her to think about meaningful ways to grow your relationship in the future.

"What's the best compliment someone has ever given you?": Not only will you learn more about what makes her feel valued, but you will also have the opportunity to compliment her yourself.

"What's one thing you love about our life right now?": Shifts the focus to gratitude and appreciating your relationship's current chapter.

"If we could design our dream date, what would it look like?": Allows her to share her ideal vision of romantic quality time, which you can make happen!

These questions are designed to spark meaningful conversations, uncover hidden thoughts, and deepen your connection in an engaging and thoughtful way.

Breaking Free from the Monotony

If your date nights have become predictable (hello, same restaurant, same order), it's time to shake things up. As guys, we can think up 20 revolutionary ideas that will turn the home woodworking business on its head. But we often struggle with finding one idea that we can do for date night. Here are some suggestions that can inject novelty, laughter, and thoughtfulness into your marriage, helping you rediscover the joy of being together.

Be Spontaneous: Surprise her with a handwritten note, plan a last-minute outing, or pick up her favorite dessert on your way home.

Have a Technology-Free Evening: Turn off your phones, laptops, and TVs for the evening and focus entirely on each other. Play a board game, have a candlelit dinner, or just talk. Removing distractions helps you reconnect and enjoy uninterrupted quality time.

Plan a Themed Night: Pick a theme – like "Hawaiian Luau," "Retro Movie Night," or "Walking Dead" and go all out with food, music, and activities to match. Themes add a playful, creative twist to an otherwise regular evening.

Work on a Project Together: Collaborate on a home improvement project, plant a garden, or even tackle a puzzle together. Shared goals foster teamwork and give you something tangible to bond over. Plus, you'll have a sense of accomplishment when it's done.

Take a Long Drive Without a Destination: Hop in the car and drive wherever the road takes you. Play your favorite music, chat, or just enjoy the silence together. The spontaneity and adventure of not having a set plan can feel freeing.

Write a Bucket List for Your Marriage: Sit down together and dream about the experiences you want to share – big or small. Whether it's traveling to a specific country, learning a skill, or attending a concert, making a list inspires excitement and keeps you both looking forward to the future.

Host a Two-Person "Dinner Party": Dress up like you're heading out for a fancy dinner but make it at home. Cook (or order) a special meal, set the table, and treat it like a date night. A change in atmosphere can make even a normal night feel extraordinary.

Revisit Old Photos or Videos: Spend an evening looking through old pictures, videos, or even love letters from when you first started dating. Reminiscing together can remind you of how far you've come and rekindle those initial sparks.

Take a Class or Workshop Together: Whether it's pottery, photography, cooking, or dancing, learning something new as a team brings energy and fun to your relationship. Plus, it gives you something to laugh about when you're both beginners.

Play Tourist in Your Own Town: Visit local attractions you've never explored, like museums, parks, or quirky restaurants. Seeing your hometown through new eyes can feel like a mini-vacation without the cost or stress of traveling.

Leave Each Other Surprise Notes: Hide little notes in places your partner will find throughout the day – on the bathroom mirror, in their bag, or on the dashboard of their car. Small, unexpected gestures of love remind them how much you care, even in the middle of a routine day.

Take a Day Off for a "Staycation": Sometimes, all you need to reconnect is a day free from obligations. Take a day off work, turn off your phones, and spend it lounging, playing board games, or exploring local attractions together. It's like a vacation without the stress of packing or travel.

Write Each Other Letters: In today's fast-paced world, taking the time to hand write a heartfelt letter can feel incredibly intimate. Express your love, gratitude, or even a funny memory. Rediscovering your partner's thoughts through written words can rekindle feelings you haven't shared in a while.

Revisit Your First Date: Relive the magic by recreating your first date. Visit the same spot, order the same food, or wear something similar to what you wore back then. It's a fun way to reflect on how far you've come as a couple while reigniting those early butterflies.

Create a "Bucket List" for the Year: Sit down together and make a list of things you want to do as a couple – big or small. Whether it's visiting a nearby town, trying a new recipe, or learning a new skill, tackling a list together keeps things exciting and goal-oriented.

Volunteer as a Team: Giving back together can strengthen your relationship by giving you a sense of purpose and shared accomplishment. Whether you're helping out at a local shelter or participating in a charity event, working as a team outside the home can strengthen your bond.

Host a Game Night – just for Two: Board games, card games, or even silly trivia can spark laughter and competition. To keep it playful and engaging, add snacks and some lighthearted stakes, like "winner picks the next vacation spot. "

Start a New Series or Book Together: Shared entertainment can give you something fresh to talk about and enjoy together. Pick a new TV series, podcast, or book and discuss it as you go. Bonus points if it sparks debates or laughter – just don't start the next episode without each other!

Overcoming Date Night Challenges

By addressing potential challenges proactively, couples can set themselves up for successful and meaningful date nights that strengthen their connection

Time Constraints: If life is hectic, plan shorter dates – like a milkshake outing or a walk. It's the quality that counts.

Budget Woes: Get creative with free or low-cost ideas. Museums often have free admission days, and cooking dinner together can be romantic and budget-friendly.

Babysitter Dilemmas: Finding reliable childcare can be a major hurdle. If babysitters are hard to come by, consider swapping date nights with another couple – you watch their kids one night, and they watch yours another. You can also have an at-home date night after the kids go to bed.

Overthinking the Plan: Trying to create the "perfect" date can cause unnecessary stress and lead to procrastination. Keep it simple – a picnic in the backyard or a pastry at a cozy cafe can be just as meaningful as a fancy dinner.

Exhaustion: After a long day, the idea of dressing up and going out can feel overwhelming. Opt for low-energy dates, like watching a movie at home or relaxing on the porch with drinks, so you can unwind while still spending time together.

Lack of Ideas: Sometimes, the hardest part of date night is coming up with something to do. Keep a shared list of date ideas handy so when the time comes, you're not stuck brainstorming.

Different Preferences: One partner may love romantic dinners, while the other prefers adventurous outings. Take turns choosing date activities to ensure both people feel their preferences are valued.

Last-Minute Cancellations: Work emergencies or unforeseen events can derail date night plans. Have a backup option ready, such as takeout or a game night, so you can still enjoy time together even if plans change.

Sticking to the Same Routine: Repeating the same date activity (e.g., dinner at the same restaurant) can make date nights feel stale. To spice things up, explore new spots, try new cuisines, or tackle an activity neither of you has done before.

Overbooking the Day: Packing your schedule too tightly before a date can leave you feeling rushed or distracted. Block out time to decompress beforehand, so you're fully present and can enjoy the experience.

Unclear Expectations: If one partner expects a grand evening and the other envisions a casual night, miscommunication can lead to disappointment. Talk about your expectations beforehand to ensure you're on the same page.

The Power of Small Gestures: Keeping the Spark Alive

Grand romantic gestures are great, but let's be real – no one has time to plan elaborate surprises every week. Luckily, small, meaningful actions can have just as much impact.

Everyday Romance

These simple but meaningful gestures can keep everyday romance alive and remind your partner how much she's loved and appreciated without overcomplicating it:

Surprise Her with Her Favorite Snack or Treat: Picking up her favorite chocolate, chips, or soda fountain drink on your way home shows you were thinking of her during the day. It's a simple way to say, "I know what you like, and I care enough to make it happen."

Warm Up Her Car on a Cold Morning: If it's chilly outside, take a few minutes to warm up her car or scrape the frost off her windshield before she leaves. It's a thoughtful way to make her day start a little smoother.

Send a Sweet Text "Just Because": A mid-day text like "Can't wait to see you tonight" or "Thinking about how lucky I am to have you" can make her feel loved and appreciated, even when you're apart.

Draw Her a Bath: After a long day, set up a relaxing bubble bath for her. Light a candle, play some calming music, and let her unwind. It's a small luxury that shows you care about her well-being.

Give Her a Genuine, Unprompted Hug: Sometimes, a heartfelt hug, given for no other reason than wanting to hold her close, speaks volumes. Physical touch is a simple but powerful way to show affection.

Surprise Her with Flowers (for No Occasion): Skip the "only on special occasions" mentality and pick up a small bouquet just because. It's a classic gesture that says, "I was thinking of you."

Create a Personalized Playlist for Her: Curate a playlist of songs that remind you of her, ones you've shared memories with, or simply tunes she loves. It's a modern, thoughtful twist on the classic mixtape.

Stealing Moments: Hold hands during a walk, sneak a kiss in the kitchen, or cuddle on the couch after the kids are asleep.

Love Languages Matter

Not all gestures are created equal. Have you ever been accused of "not trying," but in your mind, you've been bending over backward trying to make an effort? Likely, the culprit is that what you are doing is not something that resonates with her. Yes, it is important that you put in the effort. But it is so much more effective if that effort is put towards things that truly resonate with her heart.

Emotional Intimacy: The Foundation of Physical Connection

Here's the truth: physical intimacy and emotional intimacy are deeply connected. If you want to reignite the physical spark, you need to invest in the emotional side first.

Building Emotional Intimacy

Daily Check-Ins: Take five minutes a day to ask, "How are you feeling today?" and really listen to the answer.

Share Vulnerabilities: Open up about your fears, dreams, or something you've been struggling with. It might feel uncomfortable at first, but vulnerability builds trust.

Gratitude and Affirmation

Tell her what you appreciate about her. It could be as simple as, "I love how patient you are with the kids," or "You looked amazing in that dress last night." These little affirmations go a long way. We had a whole chapter on gratitude, so re-read that if you are still unsure about this concept.

ADAPTING to the Seasons of Life

Remember, romance doesn't have to look the same at every stage of life. When the kids are young, date nights might involve a babysitter and a quick dinner. When they're older, you might have more freedom to take weekend getaways. The key is to prioritize each other, no matter the season.

Laughing Your Way to Connection

I don't know about you, but the most magical sound I can ever hear in my house is the laughter of my family, especially my wife! When I can get a "guffaw" out of Jenny, I feel like Super Husband. Humor isn't just the cherry on top – it's part of the foundation of a happy marriage. Sharing a laugh can diffuse tension, boost connection, and remind you why you fell for each other in the first place.

Finding Humor in the Everyday

Look for the funny moments in daily life. Maybe it's an inside joke about how the dog only listens to her or the fact that you always forget to buy milk. Laughing together creates a bond that strengthens over time.

Activities to Spark Laughter

Watch a comedy special or a funny movie.

Share funny stories from your day, even if they're at your own expense.

Try a DIY Dance Party: Crank up some fun, upbeat music and dance like no one's watching – even if your moves are ridiculous. Laughing at your own and each other's goofy moves is guaranteed. Bonus points for re-creating iconic dance scenes (Footloose, Disco Dance Fever, Beat Street, etc.)

Attempt a "Nailed It" Cooking Challenge: Pick a fancy recipe or Pinterest-inspired dessert and try to recreate it. The inevitable mishaps – crooked cakes or undercooked soufflés – make for hilarious memories and inside jokes.

Watch or Read "Bad" Reviews Together: Find hilariously bad movie, restaurant, or product reviews and read them aloud. The exaggerated complaints and odd details can lead to side-splitting laughs.

Revisit Embarrassing Old Photos: You can pull out photo albums or scroll through old pictures and laugh at awkward hairstyles, questionable fashion choices, and funny memories. Nostalgia with a dose of humor never fails. This is especially true if you were a child of the '70s or '80s (what were we thinking???).

Write a Funny Story Together: Create a silly story where you alternate writing sentences. The plot will quickly spiral into hilarious absurdity as you build on each other's ideas.

Play the "People Watching Date Night" game: This is one of our favorite pastimes. Go to a location that is frequented by a lot of couples that (possibly) are out on dates. Observe their facial expressions, gestures, and body language to come up with a make-believe back story that explains everything you are observing. The more ridiculous, the better.

Physical Intimacy: The Real Deal for Real Men

Let's talk about physical intimacy, gentlemen. That's right, we finally get to talk about sex! It's often a topic that comes with a lot of pressure, misconceptions, and – let's be real – unspoken insecurities. Here's the good news: physical intimacy isn't about being a superstar in bed. It's about connection, trust, and pleasure *for both of you.* If romance and emotional intimacy are the foundation, physical intimacy is the fireworks display on top – but only if the groundwork is solid.

The Myths That Mess You Up

Let's tackle a few myths men often believe about sex:

Myth #1: "I need to be a sexual superhero." Newsflash: She's not judging you by your "performance" like it's an Olympic event. Women care more about connection, attentiveness, and effort than about some imaginary gold medal.

Myth #2 "She always wants to be swept off her feet.": While passion is great, not every encounter has to be a scene out of some steamy Hollywood sex scene. Sometimes, intimacy is about closeness, not grand gestures.

Myth #3 "If I last longer, it's better for her.": This myth is especially tricky because it puts pressure on you while ignoring her actual needs. Instead of focusing on the clock, focus on *her.* Listen, communicate, and pay attention to what makes her feel good.

PRACTICAL ADVICE: **Take the Pressure Off**

Sex shouldn't feel like a chore or a test. Here's how to make it happen naturally:

Ditch the "Sex-as-a-Goal" Mindset: I could stop this section right here and say, "The end." As men, we need to stop treating sex as the ultimate prize at the end of date night. Pressure kills passion. Instead, focus on being present and enjoying the moment, whether or not it leads to intimacy. If it does, how amazing is that?!? If it doesn't, that's okay, too, because we still had an amazing time together.

Create the Right Environment: A cluttered bedroom and laundry on the bed? Not sexy. Set the scene with small touches like clean sheets, candles, dim lighting, or even just a locked door if you've got kids.

Focus on Non-Sexual Touch: Hugs, holding hands, cuddling – these aren't just warm-ups for sex. They're standalone acts of love that build trust and connection. When physical affection is frequent and genuine, intimacy flows more naturally.

Be Playful, Not Pushy: Humor and lightheartedness go a long way. A spontaneous kiss, a tickle fight, or a goofy dance can lighten the mood and allow intimacy to happen without pressure.

Talking About Sex Without Awkwardness

Open communication about sex is critical, but it doesn't have to feel like an HR meeting or a high school gym class video. Here's how to make those conversations less weird and more productive:

Ask Open-Ended Questions: These questions show you care about her experience, not just your own.

"What's something you really enjoy when we're intimate?"

"Is there something new you'd like to try?"

Don't Talk About Sex... During Sex: Mid-act critiques or suggestions? Not sexy. Save the conversation for a calm, neutral moment.

Be Honest About Your Own Feelings: If you feel insecure or unsure, share it. Vulnerability deepens trust and makes it easier for her to open up, too. Be specific without assigning blame. No one tries to purposefully be bad at sex. Honor the effort. It's not that something is _wrong_; it's just that you prefer something _different_. Honest communication is especially critical when it comes to the subjects of quality and quantity. Address these issues with specificity _before_ it becomes an issue that dominates other areas of the marriage.

Write it down if you can't say it: Too embarrassed to be completely honest? Maybe she is? Start with writing things down and passing them to each other in notes. Again, be specific about needs, desires, turn-ons, and turn-offs. After a few honest and specific notes, you should start to feel more comfortable to have the same conversations verbally.

Relax, it's not that serious: In general, there is _way_ too much pressure around the topic of sex. You're a married couple in a committed relationship. Why should this topic (or any other topic, for that matter) be so taboo? It shouldn't be. Sex is one of <u>the</u> most amazing benefits of marriage! It's not just for procreation; it is also for recreation. So, get rid of the awkwardness and weirdness, and go have some fun!

Playful, Passionate, and Loving Ideas

Every couple is different, but here are some ways to spice things up while keeping it fun and loving:

Mix It Up: Routine is the enemy of passion. Change the setting, time of day, or try something new that you both feel comfortable with.

Foreplay: The Main Course, Not Just an Appetizer: Women often need more time to warm up than men. Foreplay isn't just a step in the process – it's an essential part of building connection and pleasure for her.

Non-Sexual Intimacy First: Sometimes, the most passionate moments begin with simply talking, laughing, or cuddling. Intimacy thrives on emotional connection.

Be Attuned to Her Responses: Pay attention to her body language, sounds, and expressions. If she seems uncomfortable, adjust. If she's into something, lean into it.

The Golden Rule of Physical Intimacy, "Make it about her.": No, this doesn't mean ignoring your own needs. But when you focus on her comfort, pleasure, and connection, the experience becomes more fulfilling for both of you.

The Dark Side: Pornography and Coercion

Let's address two serious threats to physical intimacy in marriage:

Pornography: Porn distorts your expectations and damages real-life intimacy. It can make you overly focused on performance and visuals, disconnecting you from your wife. It can send a catastrophic message to your wife. As porn becomes more and more prevalent (and available) in society, some studies are being released about the very disturbing (potentially permanent) effects that porn has on the male brain – even as adults. Real intimacy comes from mutual love, not a script. Stay away from porn.

Coercion: Pressuring or guilting your wife into sex isn't just wrong – it's manipulative and destroys trust. Pulling out the bible, pouting, holding her emotionally hostage for sex, etc. – it's all manipulation that has no place in a committed and loving relationship. I'll put it this way: if you have to resort to these tactics to fill your sexual needs, then YOU are failing miserably in other aspects of your marriage. Concentrate on what that is and let the sex part take care of itself. Intimacy should always be consensual and mutually desired. She's more likely to feel open to physical connection when she feels respected. Bottom line - Intimacy isn't something you take – it's something you build together.

Jenny's Comments

When I feel safe, I bring the heat. I honestly don't even know what else to say about this topic (knowing my daughter will likely read this...). Sex is a real, good, and healthy part of marriage. I have learned that this is how my husband accepts and "naturally" shows love. It's important to me to accept that love and to make sure he feels love back. But again, if I don't feel safe in my marriage, this is an impossible step to get to. But when I do feel safe, it is way more enjoyable for both of us.

Safety is created through all of the topics that Meb has mentioned. Intimacy, to me, is when we both wake up in the early morning hours (like 1-2 am) and just lay there under the covers, talking about things that are both important and unimportant. It's handholding. It's watching him eyeball-hunt for me in a crowded room and then seeing the look of relief and satisfaction in his eyes once he's spotted me. It's hearing him ask me questions about my personal self or history because he truly wants to get to know me better. It's about him needing me and only me. Safety creates closeness, connection, and a powerful interaction.

Final Thoughts

Reigniting intimacy and passion doesn't require sweeping changes – it's about small, intentional steps. Start with curiosity, sprinkle in some humor, and make space for meaningful connection. At the end of the day, intimacy isn't about grand gestures – it's about showing up for each other every single day.

Physical intimacy isn't about proving yourself or keeping score – it's about love, connection, and vulnerability. The more you focus on being present, attentive, and caring, the more fulfilling your intimate life will be for both of you. So, relax, communicate, and let the sparks fly naturally. Oh, and if nothing else works, remember: a heartfelt compliment and a back rub have magical powers. Use them wisely.

CHAPTER 6

GO ASK YOUR MOTHER, GO TALK TO YOUR FATHER

ALIGNING PARENTING AND FAMILY GOALS

If marriage is a team sport, parenting is the championship game. It's where your ability to communicate, compromise, and strategize gets put to the ultimate test. Add in sleep deprivation, school schedules, the 18 extracurricular activities (you want to letter in cornhole, how is that a thing???), the new method of learning math that makes it impossible for you to help with homework, and the occasional temper tantrum (sometimes yours), and it's easy to see how parenting can create tension.

But here's the thing: parenting doesn't have to feel like a constant tug-of-war. When you and your wife align on your goals and approach, parenting transforms from a battlefield into a partnership. You're not just surviving – you're thriving, creating a family dynamic that supports and uplifts everyone.

Finding Common Ground in Parenting Styles

No matter how much you and your wife love each other, odds are you don't agree on *everything* when it comes to parenting. Maybe one of you is a stickler for rules, while the other is more laid-back. Maybe you grew up in wildly different households and have totally different ideas about discipline, bedtimes, dating, social media, allowance, screen time, ...the list goes on.

Understanding Each Other's Parenting Philosophies

Start by having an open, judgment-free conversation about how you were raised and how it influences your parenting style. Ask each other:

- What worked well in your childhood home that you'd like to replicate?
- What didn't work that you'd like to avoid?
- What values are most important for us to teach our kids?

Understanding where you're both coming from can help you find common ground and create a unified approach.

Blending Styles

Think of your parenting styles as two pieces of a puzzle. They may not look the same, but they can fit together to create a bigger picture. If one of you is more structured and the other is more flexible, work together to find a balance. For example:

- Set clear rules and consequences but leave room for occasional leniency.
- Play to your strengths: If she's great at planning, let her handle the schedule while you focus on spontaneous fun.

Key Parenting Strategies

Communicate Away from the Kids: The phrase "Playing mom against dad" exists for a reason. Kids need consistency. Discuss parenting disagreements in private, away from the kids. This avoids confusion or playing one parent against the other while showing a united front.

Find Common Values: Focus on the core values you both agree on, such as honesty, kindness, or responsibility. Build your parenting approach around those shared principles. Even if your methods differ, shared values provide a solid foundation for decision-making that leads toward unified goals.

Alternate Decision-Making: Agree to take turns making the final call on specific parenting issues. For example, if one parent decides how to handle screen time, the other might decide on bedtime routines. This ensures that both partners feel equally respected and involved.

Use "Parenting Team Huddles": Schedule regular check-ins to discuss what's working, what's not, and how you can adjust your approach. Treat it like a strategy meeting to keep parenting on track. Open communication reduces misalignment and ensures both parents feel heard.

Respect Each Other's Strengths: Acknowledge what your partner does well, even if it's different from your approach. For example, if they're stricter, recognize that structure has its benefits. Validating each other's strengths builds trust and reduces resentment.

Pick Your Battles: Not every disagreement about parenting is worth a debate. Agree on the big issues (discipline, education) and let smaller things slide when possible. Focusing on what truly matters keeps the peace and reduces unnecessary friction.

Learn from Each Other: Instead of criticizing your partner's approach, ask questions and observe why they do things the way they do. You might find value in their methods and even adopt some of them. A little humility and curiosity can lead to better teamwork and personal growth.

Stay Flexible and Adaptable: Kids change, and so should your parenting. What works for a toddler might not work for a teenager. Regularly reevaluate your strategies and adjust as a team. Parenting isn't static, and flexibility keeps your methods effective and aligned.

Back Each Other Up in Front of the Kids: Even if you don't agree in the moment, support your partner's decision in front of the kids. Later, discuss your concerns privately. Presenting a united front shows kids that their parents are a team, which helps reinforce rules and boundaries.

Take a Parenting Workshop or Read a Book Together: Learning together from experts or parenting resources can provide a neutral ground for discussing your differences and adopting new strategies. It shifts the conversation from "my way vs. your way" to "what's best for our family."

Setting Family Goals Together: A Collaborative Approach

Family goals aren't just for New Year's resolutions. They're a powerful way to ensure everyone is moving in the same direc-tion – whether it's saving for a big trip, creating more quality time, or teaching your kids the value of kindness.

How to Set Family Goals

Gather Input: Sit down as a family and ask everyone (yes, even the kids) what they'd like to work toward.

Keep It Realistic: Aim for a mix of short-term and long-term goals. "Save for a family vacation" is great, but so is "eat dinner together three nights a week."

Write Them Down: Put your goals somewhere visible, like on a chalkboard in the kitchen or a shared calendar app.

Examples of Family Goals

- Volunteer as a family once a month.
- Plan one tech-free day every weekend.
- Teach the kids how to cook one meal by the end of the year.

The Shared Responsibility of Parenting

Parenting isn't a one-person job. When you share responsibilities, it not only lightens the load but also sets a powerful example for your kids about teamwork and equality.

Dividing Tasks

Start by making a list of everything that needs to be done, from school drop-offs to doctor's appointments to bedtime routines. Then divide and conquer based on your strengths and schedules.

- If you're an early riser, handle morning duties.
- If she's better at managing schedules, let her take the lead on planning extracurriculars.

Flexibility is Key

Life happens, and plans will change. Maybe you need to swap responsibilities for a week because of work demands, or maybe one of you needs extra support during a particularly stressful time. Be willing to adjust as needed.

Navigating Extended Family Dynamics

Let's be real: parenting doesn't happen in a vacuum. Grandparents, aunts, uncles, and other well-meaning relatives often have opinions (and lots of them). Aligning on how to handle extended family involvement is crucial for maintaining harmony.

SETTING Boundaries

Decide together how much influence extended family should have in your parenting decisions. For example:

- Are you okay with Grandma giving parenting advice, or does it need to be politely shut down?
- How do you handle relatives who spoil the kids with too many treats or toys?

Presenting a United Front

When dealing with extended family, consistency is key. If you and your wife agree on the boundaries, stick to them together. It's much easier to say no to Uncle Frank's unsolicited advice when you're on the same page.

Teaching Values and Traditions: A Joint Effort

One of the greatest gifts you can give your kids is a sense of identity rooted in shared values and traditions. These aren't just "nice-to-haves" – they're the building blocks of a strong family culture.

Identifying Core Values

Start by asking yourselves: What do we want our kids to remember about their childhood? Some examples might include:

- Compassion and kindness.
- The importance of hard work.
- Faith and spirituality.

Creating Traditions

Traditions don't have to be elaborate to be meaningful. Here are some ideas:

- Weekly family game night.
- A special birthday breakfast for each family member.
- Volunteering at a local charity every holiday season.

If you and your wife come from different cultural or religious backgrounds, find ways to blend your traditions or create new ones that reflect your values.

Aligning on Discipline

Few topics cause more tension in parenting than discipline. Whether it's time-outs, grounding, corporal punishment, or taking away privileges, it's important to align on your approach.

Establishing Rules and Consequences

Sit down together to create a list of family rules and what happens when they're broken. For example:

- Rule: No screens at the dinner table.
- Consequence: Lose screen time for the rest of the evening.

Staying Consistent

Consistency is key. If one parent enforces the rules and the other lets things slide, it sends mixed messages. Back each other up, even if you don't fully agree in the moment – you can always discuss adjustments later.

Balancing Parenting with Your Relationship

It's easy to let parenting consume all your time and energy, but don't forget – you were a couple before you were parents. Taking time to nurture your marriage is essential for maintaining a strong foundation.

Date Nights Aren't Optional

Even if it's just a quick coffee date or a walk around the block, make time for each other. Your kids will be fine without you for an hour or two.

Remember the Bigger Picture

Parenting is important, but it's not forever. Trust me when I say that someday your kids will grow up and move out, and it'll just be the two of you again. Keep investing in your relationship so that when that day comes, you'll be as connected as ever.

Jenny's Comments

Your relationship with your spouse is the best example you can set for your children on how to have a successful married life. I'm sure you've heard that saying before because it's so true! A daughter expects to be treated a certain way BECAUSE of how she saw her father treat her mother. A son looks to his dad to know how to treat women. Does his dad demean or abuse his mother, or does he treat her tenderly and with respect? This is such a gift that we can give to our kids. Their lifelong success depends on us showing up with our very best.

I suggest that you never speak negatively about your wife in front of or to your children. Not even in a joking manner. Let them see the love you have for her. Let her see them see the love that you have for her (that's a good one if you can decipher it!). Help them to treat their mother with love and kindness. This will go a long way in establishing a partnership with your wife well after the children have left the nest.

It is always endearing for me to watch how my husband fathers his daughter. I love to watch him serve her with charity and compassion. For several months, our daughter and son-in-law lived with us. Our son-in-law was completing his master's degree, and they had only one income coming in. Our son-in-law was interning throughout the United States and was gone for weeks at a time. Our daughter was working as a trauma therapist, and she worked a very stressful night shift in the center of downtown. Every night at 7 pm on the dot, my husband would walk our daughter to her car, hug her, open her car door for her, tell her to drive carefully, tell her to have a good night and be safe, and that he loved her. He would shut her car door, wait for her to drive off, and would then shut the garage door after she was safely down the road. When our daughter's husband was back in town, Meb would step aside while our daughter's husband would take over the task of seeing her off. My husband missed those nights of creating a connection with her, BUT every single morning that she returned home, at 8 am, he would be awake, welcome her home, ask her how her night was, and tell her that he hoped she would get some great sleep. I watched this play out for over a year of them living with us, and it made me feel such a stronger connection with him and a greater love for him.

Final Thoughts

Parenting isn't about being perfect – it's about being present, aligned, and willing to learn together. When you and your wife are on the same page, you create a home where your kids feel safe, loved, and supported – and that's the ultimate win.

CHAPTER 7
PUTTING THE "I" IN WE
STRENGTHENING PERSONAL
GROWTH AND DEVELOPMENT

Yes, marriage is a partnership, but it's also a journey of personal growth. The better you are as an individual, the better you'll be as a husband, father, and overall human being. It's not about being perfect; it's about striving to be better than you were yesterday.

Personal growth isn't selfish – it's an investment in your relationship. After all, your wife didn't marry you because you were static; she saw your potential. And she probably wouldn't mind if you matured enough to eventually grow out of that annoying "pull my finger" phase.

Setting Personal Goals that Complement Marital Growth

Personal goals aren't just about you – they ripple out and benefit your marriage. When you grow as a person, you bring more energy, confidence, and perspective to your relationship.

Start with Shared Values

Before setting personal goals, revisit the values you and your wife share. For example:

- If you both value health, a goal to exercise regularly or eat better complements your relationship.
- If you value financial stability, a goal to learn more about budgeting or investing aligns with your shared future.

SMART Goals for Growth

Vague goals like "be a better husband" are noble, but they're also useless without specifics. Use the SMART framework to create clear, actionable goals:

Specific: "Take my wife on a date twice a month."

Measurable: "Spend 30 minutes a day reading to improve my mindset."

Achievable: "Learn one new skill this quarter."

Relevant: "Practice active listening during conversations with my wife."

Time-Bound: "Complete a parenting book by the end of the month."

Celebrate Progress

Don't wait until you've achieved a goal to celebrate. Recognize and appreciate the small wins along the way. Share them with your wife, too – it shows her you're committed to growth.

Balancing Personal Interests with Family Commitments

Every husband needs time to recharge, but balancing these needs is delicate. You can pursue your interests without neglecting your family; it just takes intention and communication. Block out time for your hobbies, workouts, or personal projects, but keep it reasonable. If you spend more time golfing than at home, it's time to reassess.

Involving Your Family

Look for ways to combine your interests with family activities:

Love photography?: Take your wife and kids on a nature hike and capture memories.

Are you passionate about woodworking?: Involve the kids in making Fido's next doghouse. It will take twice as long, but it will mean 100x times as much.

COMMUNICATING **Your Needs**

Be honest with your wife about why personal time matters to you. For example:

"I've been feeling stressed, and I think an hour at the gym will help me decompress. Can we trade off with the kids tonight?"

This shows her you value her support while reinforcing that you're a team.

Encouraging Each Other's Passions

Supporting your wife's passions is just as important as pursuing your own. Just as you need personal time, so does she. Offer to handle dinner or bedtime with the kids so she can focus on her passions guilt-free. When you both feel encouraged to grow, it strengthens 

your bond and keeps things exciting. Take an active interest in what lights her up. Ask questions, attend events, and celebrate her milestones. Whether she's starting a side hustle, running a 5K, or taking up painting, show her that her goals matter to you. At every opportunity, brag about her in public, whether she's there or not. Trust me, the word will get back to her.

Collaborate on Shared Goals

Look for ways to align your personal growth with hers. For example:

- Take a class together (cooking, dancing, or a language).
- Set a shared fitness goal, like running a race or completing a workout program.

Continuous Learning: Growing Together

Marriage thrives when both partners are committed to lifelong learning. It doesn't have to mean going back to school (unless you want to); it's about staying curious and open to new experiences. Pick a subject or skill you've always wanted to explore, like woodworking, coding, or playing an instrument. Bonus points if it's something that benefits your family – like mastering the art of BBQ. However, it is important to remember that your likes do not have to be hers. It's great when hobbies align, but when you try and coerce your wife into developing a passion for archery, you're just setting everyone up for a hard fall.

Collaborative Learning. Find ways to learn together:

- Read a book and discuss it over breakfast.
- Watch educational documentaries and talk about what you learned.
- Take a couples' workshop on communication or parenting.

Share What You Learn

Even if you're pursuing separate interests, share your journey with each other. Talk about what you're learning and how it's helping you grow. It's a simple way to stay connected and inspired.

Overcoming Obstacles to Growth

Let's be real: growth isn't always easy. You'll hit roadblocks, get discouraged, or struggle to stay consistent. The key is to push through and keep going.

Common Challenges

Time Constraints: It's hard to focus on growth when you're juggling work, family, and other obligations. Start small – 15 minutes a day can add up.

Fear of Failure: Trying something new can feel intimidating. Remember, progress matters more than perfection.

Lack of Motivation: Share your goals with your wife and ask her to keep you accountable.

Bouncing Back from Setbacks

Missed a workout? Haven't cracked open that self-improvement book in weeks? It's okay. Growth isn't linear, and it's never too late to get back on track. Share your setbacks as well as your milestones with your wife. We're all human and – guess what – you each get to be the other's biggest motivator and cheerleader!

The Ripple Effect of Growth

When you grow as an individual, it positively impacts every area of your life – especially your marriage. You'll have more patience, energy, and confidence, which creates a ripple effect that benefits your wife and kids.

Jenny's Comments

Meb is VERY intelligent and learns concepts and skills very quickly. It's one of the reasons I fell in love with him 34 years ago and continue to be amazed by him today. He reads and watches YouTube videos about pretty much any subject, takes classes on graphic design, homesteading, farming, beekeeping, and woodworking, and even has laser etching machines in our basement. He built his motorcycle from the ground up, buying the parts as he went along and learning bit by bit, piece by piece. He's built many of the pieces of furniture in our home, as well as the gardening beds, fencing, chicken coop, and pens. He knows different styles of martial arts, knife fighting, shooting, skydiving, surfing, scuba diving, and more. He's completed his master's degree and continues to seek higher learning. He keeps up with politics and researches topics, people, and policies outside of relying on mind-numbing mainstream media. He's a wealth of knowledge and usually knows a little something about most subjects, including global current events. I take so much pride in knowing my husband is the smartest guy in the room. It makes it impossible for me to even think about straying outside my marriage because anyone else would be a total step down. I have the entire package rolled up into one God-fearing man.

However, Meb gets his happiness from spending time with me. He no longer chooses to have many outside interests and hobbies. He WANTS to do things together. He asked me to get my motorcycle license and purchase a bike so we could ride together. We work on our property together to take care of the animals and our garden. When I want to do a service project, he lovingly helps me make scratch-made meat sauce for lasagna deliveries to those in need of meals.

If you can learn together, serve together, or have mutual hobbies, then you could have so much more in common, more to talk about, and more opportunities to laugh and love.

Final Thoughts

Strengthening personal growth isn't about becoming a new person – it's about becoming the best version of yourself. And when you show up as your best self, your marriage and family life flourish.

CHAPTER 8

IT'S ALL ABOUT 'DEM BENJAMINS!

ACHIEVING FINANCIAL HARMONY

Let's face it: talking about money isn't exactly romantic. You didn't dream about balancing budgets when you exchanged vows, but financial harmony is one of the cornerstones of a strong marriage.

Money isn't just dollars and cents – it's trust, priorities, and shared dreams. When you're on the same financial page, you're not just managing resources; you're building a life together.

And when you're not? Well, those small disagreements about spending can turn into full-blown arguments.

The good news? Achieving financial harmony doesn't require spreadsheets and sacrifice (okay, maybe a little of both). It's about teamwork, transparency, and aligning your money with your values.

On this, I must admit that I am in need of much of my own advice. Because of my military background and being gone all the time, Jenny has always been our point person for all things financial. She set our budget, told me when we were broke, and told me when we could afford another one of my hair-brained ideas ("Yes honey, this Glock19 really *is* different than the last Glock19 I bought!"). Truth be told, if I was left alone tomorrow, I'd be in dire straits. I have no idea how to pay any of our bills. No clue. I don't even think I could log into our bank account.

To make matters worse, Jenny has always been the stricter of the two of us, responsible for fiscal prudence and patience. Because of her, we've always had food in the fridge, the electricity has never been shut off, and we've never had anything repossessed. I, on the other hand, have the much {{ahem}} "tougher" role of being the dreamer of the family (I know, it's a tough job, but I sacrifice for my family!). I have the next 10 years of our income already spent and am just waiting for my allowance to come in. When it's time for a big expenditure, I'm the one to say, "Let's go for it!" while Jenny has the responsibility of seeing if the numbers make sense or not.

Since retirement, I've been slowly trying to change that. It's not fair that the financial stress of bill-paying and credit card debt falls solely on Jenny's shoulders. The funny thing is that she's been doing it for so long that my efforts to help are sometimes perceived as a threat. She has a "system" that has worked for her for over three decades. When I come in and start asking "silly" questions, she can get de-fen-sive!

This is to say that we are not the gurus on this (or any other) marital topic. We are a work in progress, just like any other couple.

Creating a United Financial Vision

Before you can tackle the nitty-gritty of budgets and bills, you need a shared vision for your financial future. Think of it as the blueprint for building the life you both want.

Dream Big Together

Set aside some time to dream together about your future. Ask each other questions like:

- What does financial security mean to you?
- Where do you see us in 5, 10, or 20 years?
- What are our top priorities – buying a home, traveling, saving for the kids' education?

This isn't about numbers – it's about the big picture. Once you know what you're working toward, you can start building a plan to get there.

ALIGNING Values

Money is a reflection of what you value. If you both value family time, spending on vacations might take priority over fancy cars. If giving back is important, build philanthropy into your budget. The goal is to ensure your spending aligns with what matters most to both of you.

Budgeting for Shared and Personal Goals

If the word "budget" makes you groan, you're not alone. But think of it less like a restriction and more like a roadmap – it's how you get from where you are to where you want to be.

Building a Budget That Works

Start with the Basics: Track your income and expenses for a month to see where your money is going.

Set Priorities: Divide your budget into needs (housing, groceries), wants (date nights, hobbies), and goals (savings, debt repayment).

Include Personal Spending: Give yourselves some "fun money" to spend without guilt or questions. It's a small way to avoid feeling restricted.

Regular Budget Meetings

Once a month, sit down together to review your budget. Celebrate wins (like paying off a credit card) and adjust as needed (like trimming takeout spending if the grocery bill's getting out of hand).

OPEN COMMUNICATION About Money Matters

Financial transparency is non-negotiable. Secrets and surprises are fun for birthdays – not for bank accounts.

Schedule Money Talks

Pick a regular time to check in about finances, whether it's once a week or once a month. These conversations don't have to be long, but they should cover the essentials:

- Are we on track with our budget?
- Are there any upcoming expenses we need to plan for?
- How are we progressing toward our financial goals?

The Art of Non-Confrontational Money Conversations

Money talks can get emotional, so approach them with empathy and respect. Use "we" statements instead of "you" to keep the conversation collaborative. For example:

- "How can we adjust our spending to save more for the vacation?" is better than "You're spending too much on energy drinks."

Financial Planning for the Future

Money isn't just about the here and now – it's about preparing for the life you want down the road.

Set Long-Term Goals

Work together to set milestones, like:

- Paying off your mortgage.
- Saving for retirement.
- Building an emergency fund that covers 3–6 months of expenses.

Break these big goals into smaller, manageable steps to make them feel less daunting.

Invest in Your Future

If investing feels intimidating, start small. Consider meeting with a financial advisor to create a strategy that aligns with your goals. Even modest contributions to a retirement account or a college savings plan can make a big difference over time.

Handling Financial Setbacks Together

No matter how well you plan, life happens. A job loss, unexpected medical expenses, or a surprise car repair can throw a wrench in your finances. When setbacks occur, the most important thing is to stay united. Blaming each other will not fix the problem, but working together will. Sit down, assess the situation, and create a plan to move forward. Be willing to make temporary sacrifices to get back on track. Maybe that means cutting back on dining out or delaying a big purchase. Remind yourselves that this is a short-term adjustment for a long-term benefit.

Aligning Financial Roles

Just like in other areas of marriage, it's key to play to your strengths. One of you might be better at tracking expenses, while the other is more comfortable researching investments. Divide the responsibilities in a way that feels fair and natural.

Building Financial Trust

Trust is the foundation of financial harmony. Be honest about your spending, share your concerns, and work to create an atmosphere where both of you feel secure. If you've made financial mistakes – whether it's overspending or hiding debt – own up to them. Transparency might be uncomfortable, but it's necessary for rebuilding trust.

Celebrate Financial Wins

Celebrate your achievements, whether you're paying off a credit card, hitting a savings milestone, or simply sticking to your monthly budget. It reinforces teamwork and keeps you motivated.

Leveraging Tools and Resources

Technology can make managing your finances easier and less stressful. Here are a few tools to consider:

Budgeting Apps: Try apps like Mint or YNAB (You Need a Budget) to track your spending and savings.

Shared Calendars: Use a calendar app to plan bill payments and financial check-ins.

Online Courses: Learn more about personal finance through platforms like Coursera or Skillshare.

Jenny's Comments

I have not come out as the winner in our financial situation. If it were up to me, we'd have the equivalent of 6 months' worth of bills saved up for emergencies. We'd also have a vacation account started with a steady allotment to it, as well as a home improvement fund with steady savings in it as well. However, one big wedding, building improvements on our property, sickness and medical costs, COVID job losses, economic instability and the rise in the cost of Pretty Much Everything has affected us just as much as it has most of America. When we swing back around to making this a goal again, I hope (I know, "hope" is not a strategy!) that we will both take it seriously and contribute to building up our safety net again. Because we are working on our marriage and our communication, I'm sure we will be able to find a balance that works for us so that both of us are happy and feel safe about our financial future.

It is important to us that we choose to pay tithing to the Lord. That tithing is turned into funds that help our community members in need and go to global humanitarian efforts. We both feel strongly about giving the Lord's share back to Him. After all, He supplies everything to us all the time.

Money worries can stress a marriage. It can be the source of arguments, anger, hopelessness, and worry. If you can create a team and work together with your wife to fulfill the financial goals that both of you have, it will create much less friction to have to navigate through and will allow you both to feel like two people who are on the same team.

Final Thoughts

Achieving financial harmony isn't about having a perfect bank balance – it's about creating a life where money supports your dreams, not controls them. With open communication, shared goals, and a little teamwork, you can make your finances a source of strength in your marriage.

CHAPTER 9

AW LAWDY, THIS MARRIAGE NEEDS JESUS!

EMBRACING A FAITH-FOCUSED RELATIONSHIP

Marriage isn't just about two people – it's about the foundation you build together. And when that foundation is rooted in faith, it becomes much stronger, deeper, and more resilient. A faith-focused relationship isn't just about attending services or following rituals; it's about creating a partnership grounded in shared values, purpose, and trust in something (someone) greater than yourselves.

Faith is the glue that holds you together during life's storms, the compass that points you in the right direction, and the inspiration that inspires you to strive to be the best husband and partner you can be.

I have to stop here and say that the intention of this chapter is not to preach at or convert anyone. It is not a judgment, endorsement, or condemnation of any faith. Truth be told, I was very agnostic for nearly 25 years of our marriage. My personal belief is that it was a significant lack of a shared moral, ethical, and spiritual foundation in my own personal life that led us to the precipice of divorce. There, standing on the brink of a deep and dark abyss, I had to have a brutally honest conversation about who I was as a person, a man, a father, and a husband. I didn't like the answers that came back. It was only then that I could acknowledge that the ability to change myself at a soul-ular level would require a power much higher than anything I had to offer myself. It was through hard work and a deeply humbling process to regain some semblance of self-respect and moral rectitude that I gained a deep and unshakable belief in the spiritual faith I hold today. I have seen it work miracles in me and literally change the creature that I am. I have seen it heal Jenny and our marriage. I am in debt to my Savior, my God, and those many of my faith who ministered to Jenny and me during this dark time. Because of them, I am (we are) where we are today.

I share this with you so that you may know that this is a very deeply personal aspect of my happy marriage. I believe is absolutely essential to long-term sustainability and happiness. I am not parroting something I heard at church or believe at a surface level. It is something I've lived and experienced at a very real, very practical level. A faith-filled marriage doesn't guarantee anything. But it sure sets you up for greater success, provides a common connection, a community of cheerleaders that support healthy marital habits, and gives you a super-power resource to help when you reach into your toolbox and find it empty.

Understanding the Role of Faith in Marriage

Faith looks different for everyone, but its role in marriage is universal: it provides guidance, hope, and strength. Faith can serve as a powerful tool to strengthen a marriage, deepen connection, and provide guidance through life's ups and downs. Among many other things, faith:

Provides a Shared Moral Compass: Faith gives you a framework for making decisions and resolving conflicts based on shared principles.

Provides a Foundation for Commitment: Viewing your marriage as a sacred bond elevates your commitment to each other.

Encourages Forgiveness: Faith often emphasizes the importance of forgiveness, which is essential in marriage. It encourages letting go of grudges and resolving conflicts with compassion and understanding. Holding onto resentment can damage a relationship, but faith-based forgiveness fosters healing and reconciliation.

Promotes Humility: Faith teaches that no one is perfect and emphasizes the value of humility. This mindset helps couples admit when they're wrong and approach conflicts with openness rather than pride. Humility keeps egos in check, making compromising and growing together easier.

Provides a Shared Sense of Purpose: Faith often aligns couples with a greater purpose, whether it's serving their community, raising children with shared values, or growing spiritually together. A shared mission strengthens your bond and provides meaning beyond day-to-day challenges.

Encourages Selflessness: Many faith traditions emphasize putting others before yourself. This principle can inspire acts of kindness, patience, and love within a marriage. When both partners prioritize each other's needs, the relationship becomes more balanced and fulfilling.

Inspires Gratitude: Faith encourages thankfulness for life's blessings and for each other. Regularly expressing gratitude reinforces appreciation for your spouse. Gratitude shifts focus from what's lacking to what's abundant, fostering positivity and connection.

Offers Guidance Through Spiritual Leaders or Communities: Faith communities and spiritual leaders can provide support, wisdom, and practical advice for navigating marital challenges. Couples benefit from having a network of like-minded people and mentors to lean on for encouragement and guidance.

Teaches Patience: Faith often emphasizes the importance of patience, whether waiting for answers or enduring life's challenges. This quality can be invaluable in marriage. Patience helps you navigate disagreements, changes, and personal growth with grace and understanding.

Encourages Regular Reflection: Faith practices like prayer, meditation, or study often involve introspection, which can help couples evaluate their behavior, intentions, and relationship dynamics. Regular reflection fosters personal accountability and helps couples stay aligned with their values.

Builds Resilience in Difficult Times: Faith provides a sense of hope and strength during life's toughest moments. Whether facing financial hardship, health challenges, or loss, faith offers a source of resilience. Knowing you're part of a greater plan helps couples persevere together through adversity.

Cultivates Unconditional Love: Faith often highlights the importance of love that is not contingent on circumstances or behavior. This can inspire couples to love each other deeply and unconditionally. Unconditional love fosters acceptance and creates a safe, nurturing environment for both partners to thrive.

Exploring Faith Together

If you and your wife share the same faith, fantastic – lean into it. If your beliefs differ, that's okay, too. Focus on the common values that unite you, like love, forgiveness, and kindness. A faith-focused relationship isn't just about individual beliefs – it's about how you connect spiritually as a couple. Activities like the ones listed below not only nurture your spiritual connection but also enhance your understanding, communication, and shared sense of faithful purpose in your marriage:

ACTIVITIES TO DEEPEN Your Connection

Attend Services as a Couple: Whether it's church, synagogue, temple, or another spiritual gathering, attending together reinforces your shared commitment.

Read Together: Explore spiritual texts or devotionals as a couple. Discuss what stands out to you and how it applies to your life.

Volunteer Together: Join a service project or ministry as a couple, like helping at a food bank, mentoring youth, or participating in missionary work. Serving others reflects shared values and strengthens teamwork. Giving back as a team fosters gratitude, humility, and a deeper sense of purpose in your relationship.

Set Spiritual Goals Together: Discuss and establish goals, such as committing to daily prayer, memorizing verses, or studying a specific book of scripture. Then, work as a team toward these goals. Shared goals encourage accountability and mutual growth in your faith journey.

Celebrate Faith-Based Holidays or Traditions: Honor spiritual holidays or rituals in a meaningful way – light candles, cook special meals, or read related scriptures. Incorporate these practices into your marital routine. Observing traditions together deepens your spiritual connection and reinforces shared values.

Attend a Couples' Retreat or Workshop: To strengthen relationships, participate in a faith-based marriage retreat or workshop. These events often include discussions, activities, and spiritual teachings. Stepping away from daily life to focus on your relationship and faith can bring renewal and fresh insights.

Pray or Meditate Together: Start or end your day by praying or meditating together. It's a simple but powerful way to center your relationship.

Practice Sabbath Rest Together: Dedicate one day a week to unplugging, resting, and focusing on your faith and each other. Use the time to reflect, pray, and simply enjoy one another's company. Observing rest together allows you to slow down and prioritize spiritual and relational renewal.

Write Blessings for Each Other: Write down blessings or prayers for your spouse and share them with each other. These can be simple notes of encouragement or detailed prayers for their well-being. Speaking or writing blessings fosters gratitude and deepens your spiritual bond.

Sing or Worship Together at Home: Sing hymns, spiritual songs, or worship music together in a casual, private setting. It's a simple way to create a worshipful atmosphere in your home. Worshipping together strengthens your emotional and spiritual connection and invites peace into your home.

Reflect on Sermons or Teachings Together: After attending a service, watching a conference, or listening to a podcast, take time to discuss what resonated with you and how it applies to your relationship or family. Reflecting together encourages deeper conversations and helps you align your lives with your faith principles.

Enjoy Faith-Based Music Together: Spend time listening to or singing along with faith-based music, whether it's contemporary worship songs, traditional hymns, or instrumental pieces. Play it during car rides, while cooking dinner, or as part of a quiet evening together. Music has a unique way of uplifting the spirit and creating a peaceful, worshipful atmosphere. Faith-based music can inspire gratitude, spark meaningful conversations about your beliefs, and help you feel more connected to each other and to your faith. Plus, it's a simple way to infuse your day with positivity and joy – especially if you find a favorite song to share!

The Importance of Communicating Faith

Talk openly about your faith and what it means to you. Share your struggles, your hopes, and how your beliefs influence your perspective. This kind of vulnerability deepens your bond.

Practicing Faith-Based Traditions Together

Traditions aren't just rituals – they're meaningful reminders of your shared values and faith. If you don't already have faith-based traditions, consider creating some that resonate with both of you.

Honoring Each Other's Backgrounds

If you come from different faith traditions, find ways to honor both. Celebrate each other's holidays, incorporate elements from both traditions into your home, and create new practices that reflect your unique partnership.

Overcoming Challenges Through Faith

Faith isn't just for the good times – it's a lifeline during challenges. Whether you're facing financial stress, health issues, or a major life decision, turning to your faith can help you navigate it together. You can use faith to address conflict. By incorporating these faith-based strategies, couples can navigate conflict with greater understanding, love, and a shared sense of purpose:

Using Faith to Address Conflict

Pause and Reflect: Before reacting in anger, take a moment to pray, meditate, or reflect on your values.

Seek Guidance: Turn to spiritual texts, leaders, or mentors for wisdom.

Forgive Freely: Faith teaches us the importance of forgiveness, even when it's hard.

Pray Together Before Discussing the Issue: Start difficult conversations with a shared prayer, asking for wisdom, patience, and understanding. This sets a respectful and cooperative tone. Praying together invites humility and reminds you both to focus on resolving the conflict in alignment with your shared values.

Practice Gratitude During Conflict: When tensions rise, pause to express gratitude for one positive thing about your spouse or relationship. Acknowledging blessings helps shift the focus from negativity to appreciation, making it easier to approach the conflict constructively.

Focus on Humility, Not Blame: Faith encourages humility, so approach the conflict with a willingness to own your part instead of placing all the blame on your spouse. Humility diffuses defensiveness and opens the door to meaningful resolution.

Commit to Speak in Love: Promise each other to use kind, respectful language during disagreements, even when emotions are intense. Faith often emphasizes the power of words, reminding you to speak in ways that build up rather than tear down.

Seek Reconciliation, Not Just Resolution: Faith often prioritizes reconciliation over simply "winning" or solving the issue. Focus on restoring your connection, not just fixing the problem. Reconciliation ensures the relationship remains strong, even after the conflict is resolved.

Use Scriptural Principles as a Guide: Refer to specific teachings or stories from your faith tradition that encourage love, patience, and reconciliation. For example, "Be slow to anger" (James 1:19) or "Love is patient, love is kind" (1 Corinthians 13:4-7). Spiritual principles provide a shared foundation for resolving disagreements with compassion and fairness.

Take a Break to Pray Individually: If emotions are running high, agree to take a short break and spend it in individual prayer or meditation. This allows both of you to cool down, reflect on your role in the conflict, and return with a calmer mindset. This is my go-to "break activity" in an argument.

Practice the "Golden Rule" During Arguments: Treat your spouse how you would want to be treated in the same situation – listen attentively, avoid harsh words, and give grace. Living out the Golden Rule fosters empathy and mutual respect during disagreements.

Attend a Faith-Based Workshop or Counseling Session: If conflicts feel repetitive or unresolved, seek help through a faith-based counselor or workshop designed for couples. Professional guidance, grounded in your shared beliefs, can provide tools to address deeper issues constructively.

End Every Conflict with a Prayer or Blessing: Once the issue is discussed and resolved (or tabled for later), pray together or speak a blessing over your marriage. Ending with a positive, faith-centered moment reinforces your commitment to each other and keeps your connection strong, even after challenging conversations.

Finding Hope in Hard Times

Lean on your faith to remind you that difficult seasons are temporary. Trust that your struggles can strengthen your relationship and help you grow as a couple.

Creating a Legacy of Faith for Future Generations

Faith isn't just about you and your wife – it's about the legacy you're building for your children and future generations. Help your kids understand the importance of faith by:

- Sharing stories from your spiritual tradition.
- Modeling faith-based values like compassion, integrity, and humility.
- Encouraging them to ask questions and explore their beliefs.
- Setting the example of faith-based fundamentals like prayer, scripture reading, church attendance, service projects, etc.

Building Faith-Focused Family Traditions

Incorporate faith into your family's routines in ways that feel natural and meaningful. For example:

- Weekly family devotionals.
- A family gratitude jar where everyone writes down blessings.
- Celebrating milestones with a prayer or blessing.

Leading by Example

Your kids will learn more from your actions than your words. Show them what it means to live a faith-filled life by how you treat others, handle challenges, and prioritize your relationship with God and your family.

Cultivating a Supportive Faith Community

Faith is deeply personal, but it's also strengthened by community. Surrounding yourself with others who share your values can provide encouragement, wisdom, and accountability.

Finding Your Tribe

Look for a community where you feel comfortable and supported. This could be a church, a small group, or a network of friends who share your beliefs. Serving others is one of the most powerful ways to live out your faith as a couple. Volunteer at a local charity, participate in community service projects or find ways to support those in need.

Jenny's Comments

Meb and I studied many different religions, beliefs, and theologies before deciding on one together. We spent months reading different books and trying different methods before deciding on one that made the most sense to both of us. We chose a belief structure and church that met all our requirements. We have not regretted a single day of making that decision and have since remained steadfast in our faith.

Our friends in our faith uplift us, pray for us, and cheer us on as a couple. We do the same for them. They are there for us when we need encouragement and help. They are examples of how we want to live our own lives. They are such good people, and we love spending time getting to know them better and serving with them. We have fun together, but we also support each other's hardships.

I've seen the types of "friends" my husband has had in the past. They were not "marriage cheerleaders," nor did they care about one other's "family unit." Once Meb and I joined our faith, Meb met two men whom he started calling "friends." Their personalities were so unlike the friends I have normally seen Meb with, and they (and their wives) have been through thick and thin with us. They loved us, delivered meals when I was going through hospital stays, procedures, surgeries, and recoveries, watched our home and dogs when we had emergencies, celebrated milestones with us, were there during times of distress, and more. Meb and these other two men have a text group that is about three years old. They have solved each other's life problems in that text group. They pray for each other. They talk about how to become better men, husbands, fathers, and members of society. They talk about how to uplift and support each other. They teach each other more about the scriptures, life, and spirituality. I love the friends that my husband has now. I can't imagine a life without them in it. Does your wife feel the same about the close friends that you have chosen? Do your friends help you to be a better man and husband?

For us, joining a faith-based organization has made a huge difference in our marriage. It gives us another common goal and outlook on life. It brings us closer to one another and prompts us to be a better team.

Final Thoughts

God loves marriage! And He wants all of us to be happily married men! A faith-focused relationship isn't about perfection – it's about intention. By centering your marriage on shared values and a commitment to something greater than yourselves, you create a bond that can weather any storm. The faith-based community and support structure are important. But, in my opinion, what is critical to marriage survival and (ultimate) happiness is the strength of shared beliefs and the invitation for God to actively guide your marriage. I have never heard of a situation where He has not answered that sincere prayer.

CHAPTER 10
IT TAKES A VILLAGE TO RAISE A MARRIAGE
CULTIVATING A SUPPORTIVE COMMUNITY

You've probably heard the phrase, "It takes a village." While it's usually about raising kids, it also applies to building a strong, healthy marriage. No matter how much you and your wife love each other, you can't do it all alone. A supportive community provides encouragement, perspective, and the occasional reality check when you need it most.

Building a network of like-minded couples, friends, and mentors isn't just a "nice-to-have." It's a game-changer. It gives you people to lean on, laugh with, and learn from – and that support can make all the difference.

The Power of Peer Support: Building a Network

Having friends who "get it" can make married life feel less like a solo adventure and more like a team sport.

Why Peer Support Matters

Shared Experiences: Other couples have been through the same ups and downs, and they can offer advice, empathy, or even just a "you're not crazy" nod of understanding.

Accountability: Good friends won't hesitate to call you out when you're being stubborn or selfish. And that's a good thing.

Encouragement: When life gets tough, having a network to cheer you on can be incredibly reassuring.

How to Build Your Network

Seek Out Like-Minded Couples: Look for couples who share your values and priorities. They don't have to be exactly like you, but common ground helps.

Join Groups or Classes: Whether it's a marriage workshop, a parenting class, or a faith group, these settings are great for meeting people in similar life stages.

Invest in Friendships: Strong relationships require effort. To deepen your connections, make time for double dates, game nights, or casual meetups.

Involvement in Community and Faith Groups

Being part of a larger community provides more than just social interaction – offers opportunities for growth, support, and giving back. If you're not already involved in a community or faith group, start by exploring options that align with your interests and values. This could include:

- A men's group or couples' ministry at your church.
- A local club or organization focused on hobbies or volunteer work.
- A parenting support group for dads navigating similar challenges.

The Benefits of Group Involvement

Perspective: Hearing how others approach marriage and family life can inspire new ideas and solutions.

Accountability: Knowing others are rooting for your success helps you stay committed to your goals.

Service Opportunities: Giving back as a couple strengthens your bond and reinforces shared values.

Encouraging a Culture of Support Among Friends and Family

Your closest friends and family play a big role in your marriage. By fostering a culture of mutual support, you create an environment where everyone thrives.

Nurturing Positive Dynamics

Celebrate Together: Share milestones, successes, and happy moments with your inner circle.

Offer Help Freely: Be the kind of friend or family member who shows up, whether it's to babysit, lend an ear, or offer a helping hand.

Setting Boundaries When Needed

Not all relationships are sunshine and rainbows. If certain friends or relatives create stress or conflict, it's okay to set boundaries. Protect your marriage by limiting the influence of negative voices.

Supporting Others: The Ripple Effect

Being a supportive husband benefits your marriage and creates a ripple effect that touches your entire community. When others see you prioritizing your wife, publicly praising her, communicating with respect, and living out your values, it inspires them to do the same.

Pay It Forward

Share what you've learned with other couples. Whether it's mentoring a younger pair, offering advice to a friend in need, or simply being a good listener, your experiences can make a difference.

The Role of Humor and Positivity

I bet you'd never guess that I'm a proponent of humor! A little humor goes a long way in cultivating a supportive community.

When you're able to laugh at yourself and find the silver linings, it sets the tone for everyone around you. You don't have to be the life of the party, but bringing positivity and laughter to your relationships makes you the couple others want to be around. Celebrate the funny, heartwarming, and ridiculous moments of married life. Whether it's a silly story about trying to assemble IKEA furniture or a heartfelt anecdote about a parenting win, sharing joy strengthens your connections.

Jenny's Comments

It's not easy making new friends. Especially for introverts like us. We joined a church that is long established within this community- meaning that everybody has known each other forever. Kids grew up together, and they have been worshipping together for years. That was overwhelming, and for a second, I wondered if I would be able to fit into their world or if they would care to make "another friend." I did not wait for them to invite me anywhere (although they did consistently come over, ask me to lunch, pray for me, and spontaneously deliver a gift or a meal to my home), but rather, Meb and I started creating events at our home, so that we could invite them over and get to know them better. We had a chili cookoff competition. We held a Christmas party potluck with gifts. We go out to dinner with them occasionally. Even with their busy schedules, they let us know that they love and care about us, and we try to do the same for them. We are so grateful for their kindness, friendship, love, and support. Our friends make us want to be better, kinder, more charitable, and loving people. If you don't have friends like that as a couple, then it may be a good idea to try and find new ones!

Final Thoughts

Cultivating a supportive community isn't just about surrounding yourself with people – it's about building relationships that enrich your life and marriage. When you invest in others, they invest in you, creating a network that lifts everyone up.

With your village in place, you're equipped to face anything life throws your way – and to do it with humor, grace, and a whole lot of love.

CONCLUSION: TIME TO DROP THE MIC

YOUR NEXT CHAPTER AS A HAPPILY MARRIED MAN

Congratulations, you've made it to the end of this book – and hopefully, you didn't skim too much (I'm watching you). If you're here, it means you're serious about becoming the best husband you can be, and that alone deserves a pat on the back. Or maybe a fist bump from your wife.

Marriage is the ultimate adventure. It's equal parts joy and challenge, growth and compromise, inside jokes and deep conversations. It's also a lot of dishes, laundry, and trying to finally figure out, once and for all, where the dang remote goes when you're not watching.

This book wasn't about giving you all the answers because – let's be real – if I had all the answers, I would be too busy running sold-out marriage retreats to write this book! It was about equipping you with the tools, mindset, and strategies to build a marriage that's joyful, passionate, purpose-filled, and faith-focused.

Now, let's take a walk down memory lane and revisit the big takeaways one last time.

The Foundation: Communication Is Key

We started with communication because, frankly, it's where a lot of us guys need a little work. Marriage isn't a game of charades; it's about talking, listening, and occasionally biting your tongue when you're tempted to "fix" everything.

Remember these gems?

Active Listening: No, this doesn't mean nodding while thinking about what's for dinner. It means really listening to your wife, understanding her perspective, and maybe even taking notes (mental ones work, too).

Expressing Emotions: You learned how to use "I feel" statements instead of "You always" accusations. You're welcome.

Tackling Tough Topics: We covered how to approach difficult conversations calmly and respectfully. Hint: timing is every-thing. Don't bring up finances when she's "hangry."

If you can master communication, you'll avoid about 90% of the typical marriage arguments. The other 10% are about what to watch on Netflix, and I can't help you there.

The Unsung Hero: Gratitude

Gratitude is like WD-40 for your marriage. It smooths out the rough patches, keeps things running smoothly, and works wonders when you're in a pinch.

Daily Gratitude Rituals: Whether it's a journal, a quick "thank you," or a heartfelt conversation, showing appreciation keeps the connection alive.

Celebrate the Small Wins: Did she find your car keys again? Recognize her for it. Did you finally fix the leaky faucet? High-five yourself (and then go thank her for reminding you for six months).

Kindness is Contagious: A little kindness from you inspires a lot of kindness in return.

Gratitude shifts one's focus from what is wrong to what is right. It's a simple habit with profound results.

Balance: Work, Life, and Everything In Between

Next, we tackled the elusive concept of work-life balance. Spoiler: it's not about perfection. It's about making intentional choices to prioritize what matters most – your family, your wife, and yes, even a little time for yourself.

The highlights:

Family Time Matters: It's not just about showing up; it's about being present. Put the phone down during dinner. Your emails can wait, and your kids deserve your attention.

Boundaries Are Your Friend: Set work-free zones, learn to say no, and protect your family time like it's the last piece of pizza.

Routines Rule: Simple rituals, like morning coffee together or tech-free evenings, create connection and consistency.

Balance isn't a one-time achievement; it's a daily effort. And some days, it's okay if the scales tip a little. Just remember to adjust before things get too lopsided.

Keeping the Spark Alive

Ah, intimacy – the fun part of marriage, but also the one that often takes a backseat to life's chaos. We covered everything from rekindling emotional connection to planning creative date nights (that don't involve sweatpants and leftovers).

What to remember:

Small Gestures Matter: A love note, a compliment, or her favorite snack can go a long way. Bonus points if you remember her love language.

Plan Date Nights: No, sitting on the couch doesn't count. Get creative, get out, and maybe even get a babysitter.

Laugh Together: Humor is the secret sauce of romance. If you can laugh at the ridiculousness of life, you'll always have something to share.

Passion isn't something you "find" again; it's something you create. And good news – you now have the tools to do it.

Growing Together and Individually

Personal growth isn't just about you – it's about showing up as your best self for your wife, your kids, and your marriage.

Key points:

Set Personal Goals: Whether it's learning a new skill or finally organizing the garage, growth keeps you energized and confident.

Support Each Other's Passions: Cheer her on, create space for her hobbies, and celebrate her wins.

Learn Together: Whether it's a new language, a cooking class, or a parenting workshop, shared growth deepens your connection.

You don't have to be perfect. You just have to keep moving forward.

Finances: Love and Money

Talking about money isn't exactly romantic, but it's essential. Financial harmony creates stability, reduces stress, and frees you up to focus on what really matters.

The big takeaways:

Communicate About Money: No secrets, no surprises, and no blaming each other for Amazon purchases.

Set Shared Goals: Whether it's paying off debt, saving for a vacation, or investing in the future, make a plan together.

Celebrate Wins: Hitting a financial milestone deserves more than a pat on the back. Maybe even splurge on a fancy date night.

Money talks don't have to be stressful. They can be empowering, especially when you approach them as a team.

Grounding Your Marriage in Faith

Faith adds depth and meaning to your marriage, giving you a foundation to lean on when life gets tough.

Highlights:

Shared Faith Practices: Praying together, attending services, or reflecting on spiritual texts strengthens your bond.

Finding Hope in Challenges: Faith reminds you that struggles are temporary and growth is possible.

Creating a Legacy: By modeling faith and values, you're not just shaping your marriage – you're shaping the next generation.

Faith isn't about perfection; it's about direction. And when your marriage is centered on something greater than yourselves, it becomes unshakable.

Your Support System

Marriage doesn't happen in a vacuum. Surrounding yourselves with supportive friends, family, and community is the secret weapon for long-term success.

Remember:

Find Your Tribe: Build a network of like-minded couples and friends who encourage and inspire you.

Lean Into Community: Whether it's a faith group, a parenting circle, or a bowling league, community enriches your life.

Pay It Forward: Share what you've learned with others. Your story and experiences can inspire someone else's journey.

No couple is an island. The stronger your village, the stronger your marriage.

Jenny's Comments

I'm happy to report that our marriage is stronger today than it has ever been. We have our off days. We have our down days. We even have the dreaded, horrible fight now and then. But now that we know how good our life can be together, we don't want to sacrifice even a minute to stay mad. Now, one of us comes up to the surface, realizes what's more important, and then throws a buoy to the other. When we both can breathe again, we look at each other and are able to gain traction again, back on the path of a healthy marriage.

Please don't let your marriage suffer one more unnecessary minute. If you have the ability to do something about it, why not take the leap of faith and reach out to your wife and see if you can salvage your marriage if it's in jeopardy, get closer if you are in "roommate status," or reach unexpected heights as best friends and lovers. Mutual respect, communication, building a friendship, and making meaningful memories together all help in building a life that you can love with your spouse! Even if you pick just one thing today out of this book you can try – why not give it a shot? What's the worst that could happen?

Your Next Steps

You've got the tools. You've got the strategies. Now it's time to put them into action. Start small - maybe with a handwritten note of appreciation or a date night on the calendar. Then keep building, one step at a time.

Remember, marriage isn't about being perfect. It's about being present, intentional, and willing to grow. The fact that you've read this far means you're already ahead of the game.

So go on - be the happily married man you were meant to be. Love big, laugh often, and never stop learning. The best is yet to come.

Make a Difference with Your Review

You know that feeling when you hold the door for someone, and they light up with a big smile? Leaving a review for our book is kind of like that—but even better. You won't just brighten someone's day—you might change their life.

Would you help someone searching for hope, joy, and purpose in their marriage but unsure where to begin?

Our mission with *The Art of Being A Happily Married Man* is to provide real, practical tools that husbands can use every day. But to reach more husbands, we need your help.

By leaving a review, you're not just sharing your thoughts—you're helping a fellow husband or wife on their journey toward a stronger, more joyful marriage.

It costs nothing, takes less than a minute, but could make a lasting impact. Your review could help…

…one more couple laugh together again.

…one more family build a legacy of love.

…one more person realize they're not alone.

To make a difference, simply scan the

QR code or click the link.

Click Here to Review The Book On Amazon

If you love helping others, you're our kind of person. Thank you from the bottom of our hearts! - Meb & Jenny West

RESOURCES

Algoe, S. B., Gable, S. L., & Maisel, N. C. (2010). It's the little things: Everyday gratitude as a booster shot for romantic relationships. *Personal Relationships, 17*(2), 217-233. https://doi.org/10.1111/j.1475-6811.2010.01273.x

Bach, D. (2002). *Smart couples finish rich: 9 steps to creating a rich future for you and your partner.* Crown Business.

Baumrind, D. (1991). The influence of parenting style on adolescent competence and substance use. *The Journal of Early Adolescence, 11*(1), 56-95. https://doi.org/10.1177/0272431691111004

Cann, A., & Calhoun, L. G. (2001). Perceived personality associations with differences in sense of humor: Stereotypes of hypothetical others with high or low senses of humor. *Humor, 14*(2), 117-130. https://doi.org/10.1515/humr.14.2.117

Chapman, G. (2015). *The five love languages: The secret to love that lasts.* Northfield Publishing.

Cloud, H., & Townsend, J. (1992). *Boundaries: When to say yes, how to say no to take control of your life.* Zondervan.

Covey, S. (1997). *The 7 habits of highly effective families.* St. Martin's Press.

Dew, J. (2007). Two sides of the same coin? The differing roles of assets and consumer debt in marriage. *Journal of Family and Economic Issues, 28*(1), 89-104. https://doi.org/10.1007/s10834-006-9051-6

Eggerichs, E. (2004). *Love & respect: The love she most desires; the respect he desperately needs.* Thomas Nelson.

Fay, C., & Cline, F. (1990). *Parenting with love and logic: Teaching children responsibility.* NavPress.

Godin, S. (2008). *Tribes: We need you to lead us.* Portfolio.

Gottman, J., & Silver, N. (2015). *The seven principles for making marriage work: A practical guide from the country's foremost relationship expert.* Harmony Books.

Goulston, M. (2015). *Talking to crazy: How to deal with the irrational and impossible people in your life.* AMACOM.

Gray, J. (1992). *Men are from Mars, women are from Venus: A practical guide for improving communication and getting what you want in your relationships.* HarperCollins.

Greenhaus, J. H., & Powell, G. N. (2006). When work and family are allies: A theory of work-family enrichment. *Academy of Management Review, 31*(1), 72-92. https://doi.org/10.5465/amr.2006.19379625

Hall, J. A. (2013). Humor in long-term romantic relationships: The association of general humor styles and relationship-specific functions with relationship satisfaction. *Western Journal of Communication, 77*(3), 272-292. https://doi.org/10.1080/10570314.2012.757796

Harley, W. (2011). *His needs, her needs: Building an affair-proof marriage.* Revell.

Journal of Family and Economic Issues. Various articles on financial stress and its impact on relationships.

Journal of Personality and Social Psychology. Various articles on gratitude in relationships.

Julien, D., Markman, H. J., & Lindahl, K. M. (1989). Interactional dimensions of social support in marriage: A descriptive and methodological analysis. *Journal of Family Psychology, 3*(1), 53-67. https://doi.org/10.1037/h0080528

Mahoney, A., Pargament, K. I., Murray-Swank, A., & Murray-Swank, N. (2003). Religion and the sanctification of family relationships. *Review of Religious Research, 44*(3), 220-236. https://doi.org/10.2307/3512384

Markham, L. (2012). *Peaceful parent, happy kids: How to stop yelling and start connecting.* Perigee Books.

Markman, H. J., Stanley, S. M., & Blumberg, S. L. (2010). *Fighting for your marriage: A deluxe revised edition of the classic best-seller for enhancing marriage and preventing divorce.* Jossey-Bass.

McKeown, G. (2014). *Essentialism: The disciplined pursuit of less.* Currency.

Perel, E. (2017). *The state of affairs: Rethinking infidelity.* HarperCollins.

Pew Research Center. (2021). Parenting in America: Outlook, worries, aspirations are strongly linked to financial situation. *Pew Research Center.* Retrieved from https://www.pewresearch.org.

Ramsey, D. (2013). *The total money makeover: A proven plan for financial fitness.* Thomas Nelson.

The Holy Bible. (Various Editions). Verses on marriage include: Proverbs 18:22; Ecclesiastes 4:9-12; Ephesians 5:25-33.

Thomas, G. (2015). *Sacred marriage: What if God designed marriage to make us holy more than to make us happy?* Zondervan.

ABOUT THE AUTHOR

Meb and Jenny have been married for over 33 years. Their enduring partnership, built while raising their now-married adult daughter, is grounded in a faith in God and a firm belief in the sanctity of marriage - values they have learned to embrace through significant hardships. From financial struggles to long separations during multiple military deployments, Meb and Jenny learned to prioritize faith, commitment, communication, and growth to build a marriage that has withstood the tests of time.

Meb is a seasoned security consultant, business continuity manager, and author with over 35 years of professional experience. A retired U.S. Army Senior Leader and Ranger with 26 years of service, he has navigated high-stakes challenges in global conflicts, honing expertise in leadership, resilience, and strategic problem-solving.

Jenny is also a seasoned security consultant, award-winning small business owner, veteran, and military spouse. She has served her community and her family around the globe, leaving a lasting impact everywhere she went. Most of all, she's the bomb.com when it comes to being a Super-Mom and a stone-cold-foxy wife.

In *The Art of the Happily Married Man*, Meb blends his professional expertise and unparalleled sense of humor with personal stories from his marriage. He shares lessons learned through challenges, offering practical strategies, encouragement, and wisdom for men looking to strengthen their relationships. With a focus on faith, communication, and resilience, Meb's inspiring voice guides readers to build joyful, steadfast, fulfilling, and lasting marriages. Jenny comments throughout the book to keep Meb in check and the readers on track.